# Twelve-Key Practice

## THE PATH TO MASTERY & INDIVIDUALITY

# Julie Lyonn Lieberman

*Designed for All Instruments & All Styles in Triple Clef*

*Twelve-Key Practice:*
*The Path to Mastery and Individuality*
by Julie Lyonn Lieberman

Designed by Julie Lyonn Lieberman
Published by Julie Lyonn Music

Distributed by:
Hal Leonard Corporation

Copyright © 2019 Julie Lyonn Music
First Printing 2019
Printed in the United States of America

Library of Congress Cataloging in Publication Data
Lieberman, Julie Lyonn
*Twelve-Key Practice:*
*The Path to Mastery and Individuality*

by Julie Lyonn Lieberman
Includes index
1. Bowed Strings 2. Violin 3. Viola 4. Cello
5. Flute 6. Clarinet 7. Alto Saxophone 8. Trumpet 9. Piano 10. Guitar
11. Music 12. Musicians 13. Creative Musicianship 14. Transposition
15. Twelve Keys 16. Improvisation 17. Composition 18. Paradiddles
19. World Scales 20. World Rhythms 21. Riffs

# Contents

# Acknowledgments

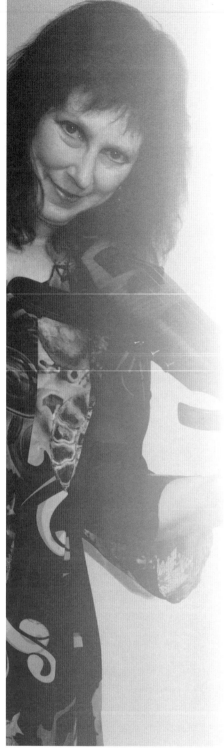

It's a tremendous undertaking to write, notate and design a book. Over the years, I have had the great fortune to meet and build co-creative relationships with talented and supportive compadres.

I am grateful to writer **Carrie Ann Lahain** for her editing advice throughout the writing process.

Many thanks to graphic designer **Loren Moss Meyer**, who started out as my student in New York City many decades ago and became a good friend and design mentor.

Special thanks to my husband and fur-child for their patience over the long hours spent working on *Twelve-Key Practice*.

I deeply appreciate endorsement quotes from such an awesome group of creative artists:

◇ Saxophonist and jazz educator, **Jamey Aebersold**.

◇ Violist, author, and educator, **David Wallace**.

◇ Composer and pianist, **William Healy**.

◇ Jazz guitarist, composer and author, **Rez Abbasi**.

◇ Grammy-nominated clarinetist, composer, performer and educator, **David Krakauer**.

# A Note to My Readers

Imagine you could hear a musical phrase, picture its layout on your instrument by "seeing" and "feeling" the fingerings and/or embouchure in your mind's eye, know the names of the notes, and hear the dynamics you want to include. All simultaneously, in a millisecond, and without moving a muscle! Welcome to the Twelve-Key approach.

This book reflects close to half a century of study, practice, and teaching. Twelve-key practice certainly isn't a unique idea and is particularly prevalent in jazz training. It's just never been sequenced or taught through the lens offered within these pages. The exercises in this book span a number of styles, brain skills and practice techniques—all presented using a kaleidoscopic learning style.

Before journeying into jazz and world music in my early twenties, I studied with five different classical violin teachers each with a different orientation to instruction. And yet, every new teacher except one paired a scale and arpeggio with a piece of music in that same key, starting with the easiest key on my instrument and progressing sequentially from there. This tried and true approach to pedagogy certainly made sense to me at first.

My earliest teacher was Samuel Applebaum, author of the *String Builder* series. The second teacher, Nancy Clarke of the Curtis Institute, used the most prevalent etude books to predate Applebaum's method. It was only my third of the five classical teachers, Romuald Tecco, a Galamian acolyte, who introduced me to arpeggios and scales in all twelve keys.

I did not learn to make the twelve keys my own from Galamian's book, *Contemporary Violin Technique*. I stood at a music stand and followed the fingerings my teacher had hastily penciled in. As trained, I translated the symbols on the page into muscle moves. I did not hear what I saw until after the fact. Not one of my teachers had taught me to even try. I breezed through the keys I'd already encountered in earlier exercises, and certainly, there were moments when I squirmed inside while playing the keys that felt as though they didn't belong on my instrument. Keys like F# and Db were foreign and uncomfortable. Each time the book closed, so did my awareness of those squirmy keys. I reasoned this practice would prepare me for concertos in various keys.

> Scales and arpeggios are such a small fraction of how the musical imagination dances between and through the notes.

This was my only encounter—and not a useful one—until I studied jazz for eight years with jazz pianist Sal Mosca, a protégé of the founder of the cool jazz movement, Lennie Tristano. My jazz studies were practiced by ear rather than the visual-only approach applied during my classical training. Yet, this was still a limited learning experience. Yes, the keys were instilled into muscle and auditory memory. And yes, I finally learned my key signatures such that the knowledge was accessible at all times. But scales and arpeggios are such a small fraction of how the musical imagination moves from note to note. It wasn't until I was invited to perform at a healing arts festival in New York in the early 1980s, where I met a protégé of Ravi Shankar, sitarist Roop Verma, that I began to perceive mastery of the notes in each key with a fresh perspective.

I was working on the East meets West chapter for my book, *Improvising Violin*, and Roop graciously granted me an interview. His explanation, when asked how to prepare to improvise on a raga, later became fodder for my exercises, "Rhythmic and Pitch Permutations." I later presented this information in workshops and finally, in my 2016 Hal Leonard book, *How to Play Contemporary Strings*. I have woven the practice system into this book.

Roop said, "Julie, I practice every possible combination of two, three, four, five, six, then seven notes of the scale for each raga I plan to perform. All by ear." When I asked how long this took him, he replied, "At least one week per scale. And that's just the first time through." That single conversation pointed my attention to an entirely new way to map and practice the scope of possibility on my fingerboard.

If you've ever played Boggle, the East Indian approach to practice is a bit like that. Instead of only perceiving the notes in the order named and/or practiced, like C D E—which is a linear, sequential left-brain cognitive process, you train your brain to perceive every possible combination of those three notes. For instance, C D E would be practiced as follows:

I apply this system to how I practice in all twelve keys every day. I also rotate material. If I play minor pentatonic scales on Monday, dominant seventh chords on Tuesday, major pentatonic on Wednesday, and a pattern that emphasizes the sixth of the key on Thursday, then today I might scan Youtube for a sax or piano solo, wait until I hear a magical phrase, learn it, and move it through the twelve keys. Then, it's onwards to diminished, augmented triads, another "borrowed" pattern—always consciously choosing riffs from a balance of instrumentalists inside and outside my wheelhouse. I am also careful to include rhythmic content from a wide range of genres whenever possible, so I don't spend the bulk of my practice time on symmetrical rhythms like quarter and eighth notes.

The practice material offered in this book will require hard work but will also yield amazing gains. I look forward to hearing about the ideas you incorporate into your own twelve-key regimen as you develop a personal vocabulary of musical phrases for twelve-key practice.

# Overture ♭♭♯

## THE BENEFITS OF THE TWELVE-KEY APPROACH

Any practice system can enable you to improve, but which skills will you strengthen and to what degree? The Twelve-Key Approach will teach you more than how to develop an evenly distributed proficiency in all twelve keys. That's because this book provides step-by-step practice material designed to build far greater skill than physical prowess on your instrument. You will learn how to generate a well-balanced cooperation between the musical learning centers of your brain. The heightened state of awareness you'll achieve through the Twelve-Key Approach will provide a new perceptual support system designed to help you discover your own unique voice on your instrument.

> Twelve Key Practice applies the latest breakthroughs in brain biomechanics to facilitate technical mastery. This serves the ultimate goal: Musical Excellence and Heightened Artistry.

There are probably 20,000 guitarists in New York City alone who can spit out memorized riff after riff rather than innovate their own musical language. Mindless physical repetition limits potential. Mindful practice will enable you to design an exclusively personal practice system. In fact, this unique system will enable you to distinguish yourself from players who tend to practice the same cookie cutter techniques and repertoire in the same order. You will discover surprisingly shadowy areas within your physical and mental skills—even in keys you thought you'd mastered—as you cultivate every possible perceptual and physical strategy suggested in this book to move patterns and phrases through the twelve keys.

Music pedagogy most commonly teaches us one skill-set at a time. This makes sense but, beyond the initial exertion required to master each new skill, it inadvertently encourages musicians to apply mindless repetition to practice. Repetitive practice is used to instill new skills and repertoire into muscle memory. Though muscle memory is useful to a certain extent, it ultimately doesn't serve the musical artist fully if relied upon above all other skills. **Muscle memory is the first to go** when the body floods with what I refer to as "the chemistry of nervousness." At least twenty organic chemicals are activated by stress—not just adrenaline. If you haven't engaged the other music learning centers of the brain during the training process, good luck to you when under pressure!

Through the whole-brain practice approach offered in this book, you will ultimately command a rich array of skills as you learn to become the true driver at the wheel during practice and performance.

# BRAIN DOMINANCE AND ITS EFFECT ON MUSIC-MAKING

Our brains were built to seek economy of motion, so it's common to unconsciously avoid a mental strategy that demands a full state of wakefulness. It would be natural, then, to be attracted to warm-up exercises that feel comfortable and avoid exerting your brain full throttle. If you are willing to give the Twelve-Key Approach a try, you'll develop a level of mental stamina and alertness that will serve you musically as well as in other areas of your life.

It's estimated that the brain consists of about 100 billion neurons. Each neuron can generate roughly 10,000 connections with its counterparts. To make this easier to picture, think of your brain like the command center at Grand Central Station: Each track has a purpose and a destination—outgoing, incoming, or both—and your intention helps determine which track will activate at what time, its pace, and the overall map for how it progresses.

How you practice is just as important as what you practice.

For any number of reasons, you may have unconsciously favored certain train tracks over others. Mental habits are often fed by early educational experiences—familial and classroom learning—mixed with a touch of genetics. But the muscles of the body and the neural networks of the brain, unlike the equipment at a train station, can weaken without use and won't be able to instantaneously perform at full capacity when needed. A weaker "muscle" will always allow the stronger one to take over which will, in turn, become even stronger. Therefore, it's a given that whichever mental skills you use most will overshadow other potentially productive learning and command capabilities.

Twelve-key practice is about so much more than learning to play in all twelve keys.

To clarify this concept even more, let's use an F scale as an example. If you practice it every day, all year long, it shouldn't surprise you when it's easier to play a composition or improvisation in the key of F. Nor would it be astonishing if you stumble or play out of tune in a key you haven't practiced. There is good news here. Just as you can strengthen weak muscles, you can also change, and in this case balance, mental hierarchy by strengthening your weaker skills.

You will also learn how to monitor your brain activity: If your brain tends to fall asleep and, depending on your instrument, allows the fingers, tongue or lips to move automatically rather than with artistic direction, you will be able to apply the protocol outlined in this book to reinvigorate full engagement. This process will help build mental stamina and foster skills that boost your craft to amazing heights.

If you've ever worked with a trainer at a gym, then you already know the same workout every day, no matter how demanding, will gradually decrease in benefit until it provides little or no value. For that reason, the Twelve-Key approach has been designed to present constant and ever-changing mental and physical challenges while you master any given phrase in all twelve keys. Each time muscle memory takes over and your other mental "muscles" go to sleep, you will have the tools you need to wake up "the team" and put it to work.

Whether you're primarily a reading musician or an improviser, learn how to steer your mental hierarchy from one that activates and mostly relies on a few unconscious learning skills as your command center—whether it's your eyes, ears or muscle memory—to one that balances the use of the entire musical brain: the auditory, kinesthetic, imagistic and analytic. More about that in a moment!

The biggest challenge in this book might not be the exercises themselves, but how you hold the material in your brain and ears.

# How to Proceed

This book is designed in a non-linear fashion. Feel free to pick the section that calls out to you.

I do highly recommend you familiarize yourself with the four approaches that particularly define twelve-key practice as a prelude to approaching the material in this book. You will find details in the next chapter, "The Twelve-Key Approach."

- ⋄ The Scale Degree Numbering System.

- ⋄ Trilateral Learning: A whole-brain learning approach.

- ⋄ Kaleidoscopic Layering: The engagement of multiple learning tactics.

- ⋄ Directional Practice: How to bypass linear thinking and strengthen your mental map for each exercise.

As is the case with any new practice system, a few minutes a day with full concentration is better than "I'll get to it later when I have a huge chunk of time…"

There's a lifetime of practice material in this book. Enjoy!

# Getting Started

## SCALE DEGREE NUMBERING SYSTEM

Whenever possible, a numbering system that identifies the degrees of the scale will be used rather than note names or notation. This procedure will enable you to begin to perceive the intervals between pitches and their relationship to the key signature or chord changes, rather than either the translation of dots into muscle moves if reading music, or parroting what you hear if learning by ear. An understanding of inter-relationships between notes will provide the scaffold upon which you can accelerate your learning process and improve your interpretation or creation of melodic ideas.

All you will need is just **ONE** sequence of numbers to play each phrase or melody in all 12 keys.

For instance, the C major and the C natural minor scales would normally be represented like this:

The numbering system will look like this:

**Major Scale:** R 2 3 4 5 6 7 8

**Natural Minor Scale:** R 2 ♭3 4 5 ♭6 ♭7 8

What's different about using a numbering system? You have to think about the note names as you picture or map the pitches on your instrument. Notation for jazz chords uses Roman Numerals. For instance, if you want to convey a D minor chord that moves to a G7 chord and resolves on a C major chord, it will look like this: **ii V7 I**

The lower case denotes minor, upper case signifies major, and the "7" next to the V chord indicates a dominant seventh chord, a major triad with a flatted seventh on top: **R 3 5 b7**

The numbering system for degrees of the scale employs regular integers.

Here's a melodic phrase in the key of C:

Here's the phrase again, but with the degrees of the scale. We will use boldface to communicate a pitch that drops below the root of the key: 1 8 3 4 b5 5 **5 5**

There's something missing, isn't there? The rhythm! Throughout this book, I will provide you with rhythmic content in tandem with the degrees of the scale. It's harder work. You will have to learn the rhythms separately first, decipher the pitches, and then join the two together.

## THE TRILATERAL LEARNING SYSTEM

As you work on the exercises in this book, you will have an opportunity to train yourself to activate and balance three learning centers. Muscle memory isn't listed in this system. That's because, once you initialize physical motion, particularly when repetitive, the motor cortex will automatically perform its job to imprint those muscle moves into auto-response. Do you have to stop and think about how to open your instrument's case anymore? No, muscle memory performs the task automatically based on dozens, hundreds or thousands of repetitions.

However, the following three learning centers are crucial to musicianship and do require intentional activation on your part.

⋄ **Analytical:** The ability to look at or hear a musical passage and understand the scaffolding upon which it has been built, such as how the notes relate to the key, to the chords, and to the overall length and organization of the passage, how the melody does or doesn't cadence, notes that are outside the key, and any other pertinent details.

- **Imagistic:** The ability to visualize yourself practicing your instrument without moving your body. If you can get up out of a chair and walk across the room without moving a muscle, then you can use this part of the right brain to map the note-to-note spatial relationships on your instrument.

- **Auditory:** The ability to hear the melody in the inner ear separate from playing it on your instrument. You can test this skill by whistling or singing a melody you've just practiced.

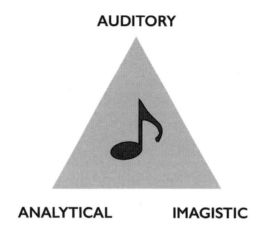

## HOW DO WE NORMALLY LEARN MUSIC?

The three most common approaches to learning music are:

- Read the piece over and over until you can turn from the music stand and still "see" the sheet music in your mind's eye.

- Lock the melody into your inner ear, referred to as audiation.

- Imprint the fine-tuned navigational skills required to play the piece into muscle memory through repetitive practice.

Imagine you want to lift up something heavy. Instead of planting both feet symmetrically, what if you stood on one foot and only used three fingers of your non-dominant hand? If the learning procedures you use are missing a number of crucial components, don't feel surprised if you blank out on sections of the music you thought you knew so well. As mentioned earlier, there are at least three primary learning centers—auditory, analytic, and imagistic—that can put you on solid ground while automatically cultivating muscle memory.

Let's explore the strengths and inherent problems that accompany the most common, but insufficient, learning processes.

───────

### Visual

The visual cortex consumes a lot more real estate than the auditory cortex. And we use the visual cortex in modern life beyond that of our ancestors because of the advent of computers, smart phones, video games, and the like. In my 1991 publication, *You Are Your Instrument*, I wrote about research which determined when we use our eyes, our other senses shut down as much as 75%! This is not good news for the reading musician.

In addition, when we read music, our eyes move in a linear, sequential pattern to convert symbols into muscle moves. This activates the left brain. Mapping, i.e. tracking spatial relationships, is commandeered by the right brain. And the auditory section of the brain can be found in yet another area of the cortex. How ironic. When you use your eyes to play, your brain is annexing valuable energy needed to make music.

You could argue that playing music is a whole brain activity, and that's true. But given how much brain area is dedicated to the visual cortex, do you really want to set up a hierarchy that activates your visual cortex as the primary control center over your other senses?

---

## Muscle Memory

The use of repetition to master exercises and pieces of music such that your muscles can perform the riff, phrase or piece while you think about something else can certainly be useful. There's no reason why you should have to learn everything from scratch each time you pull out your instrument. However, **excessive repetition can invite injury**. More importantly, **muscle memory can likely fail you** when the body is flooded with over twenty chemicals before a performance, recital or lesson—yes, far more than the simplified explanation that only mentions adrenaline. Even fatigue or anxiety can weaken or wipe it out.

Isn't it bewildering when a piece of music you thought you knew so well suddenly vaporizes? Or, you find you have to play the opening to the piece a number of times to get a running start into a section that eludes you?

There are some other problems inherent in dependency on muscle memory. When you memorize a phrase, it's more common to lock the melodic/rhythmic sequence into your ears as one single cloth, followed by repetitious practice to imprint that phrase into your muscle memory. The Twelve-Key Approach aspires to teach rhythm and melody as separate learning processes. Also, during this repetitious process, you are actually building something called a sensory engram. This engram can be found in your motor cortex and behaves like a barcode. It tracks every detail concerning the specific coordinated muscles moves essential to that phrase. If, incidentally, you hold your breath during practice and flex your right big toe, the sensory engram will act like a kinesthetic tape recorder and weave those muscular settings into the overall engram so that every time in the future you play that phrase or piece of music, you will most likely hold your breath and/or flex your right big toe.

Your body does not play your instrument. Your brain is the command center that tells your body what to do.

## Aural or Auditory

It's essential to be able to hear any piece you work on in your inner ear without touching your instrument. But you'd have every reason to feel nervous before and during a performance if you only relied on that skill. Look at this through a different lens: If I show you a picture of a lake and tell you the name of the lake and even the name of the town and state it's in, that doesn't mean you'll know how to travel there. If you learn each piece of music solely by ear, that's a big win, because music is, after all, an aural art form. But your brain will require more scaffolding to support you, particularly in pressured situations. This is because **if you can hear how the piece should go but your fingers, tongue or lips stumble and you have no other skill to fall back on**, moments like these can ruin the quality of experience I assume you would like to have while playing.

## MENTAL SKILL QUIZ

**Let's try a few quick tests to figure out which mental muscle(s) you use most frequently:**

- ◇ Play a musical phrase from a melody you learned fairly recently. For our purposes, choose something that isn't much longer than two measures.

- ◇ Next, whistle, hum or sing the melodic phrase or melody from start to finish to determine whether you have locked it into the auditory memory center of your brain.

- ◇ Mime playing the phrase with only your left hand. As you do this, picture what the right hand would be needed for but don't move it.

- ◇ Repeat the phrase again using only your right hand. As you do this, picture what the left hand would be needed for but don't move it.

- ◇ Now strip out the rhythmic values in the phrase and play the notes in proper order as walking quarter notes.

- ◇ Strip out the pitches and tap, clap or drum the rhythms.

- ◇ Play an entire piece from memory but don't physically play every single note. Drop in and out in random sequence. During the moments when you aren't playing, don't move a muscle in your body. Instead, hear and image the notes on your instrument so that you can seamlessly re-enter the piece at whatever moment in the music you choose without dropping a beat.

- ◇ Sing the melody while naming the pitches.

- ◇ Sing the melody while naming the fingerings.

- ◇ Play the melody either an octave lower or higher. If your instrument accommodates both, try each. Without an understanding of the scaffold that binds the melody to the key or chord changes, this will be difficult unless you have perfect pitch.

What did you learn about yourself? Which skills came easily, and which were a struggle? If you're interested in developing balanced music-making skills, your findings will inform future practice sessions. Can't hear the rhythms without the melody? Don't have a clue what one hand should be doing while the other hand's responsibilities are crystal clear? Can't picture how your embouchure should function for part of the phrase if you're a wind player? That's what you need to practice.

**Here are a few suggested approaches to learning music at the music stand:**

- ◇ Choose a short musical phrase. Practice hearing it in your inner ear as you read it. Try to whistle or hum it before you play it.

- ◇ Play a small section of a piece of music a few times to lock it into your ears. Make a mental note of how the phrase encircles or quotes notes from the arpeggio per the key signature. For instance, if the piece of music is in the key of A, and the melody starts on an E and moves to a C♯, those are two primary notes in the key. Now use what you've learned about the phrase to attempt to play it from memory.

- ◇ Record a new piece section by section. Repeat each phrase a couple of times but leave enough beats in between each rendition to match phrase length so you can practice learning the piece by ear via call and response during playback. Consider adding a few beats to give yourself adequate time to apply Trilateral Learning to it as well.

# An Overview of The Twelve-Key Approach

The Twelve-Key approach is based on a learning system that balances three mental skills in particular:

- **Audiate the pitch sequence and the rhythmic sequence** as separate events and as a single event.

- Practice the Melodic Map:  **Visualize playing the notes without touching your instrument** a millisecond before you play each phrase.

- Envision the scaffold: Whenever possible, **visualize the harmonic and theoretical framework** that glues the notes in a phrase together.

Once you've locked the pattern or melodic phrase into your three primary learning centers then apply kaleidoscopic learning to how you practice:

- Notice the interval between the first and last notes of the phrase.

- Notice the interval-to-interval motion between each of the notes in the phrase.

- Notice how the pitches apply to or weave around the notes of the major or minor arpeggio (or chord tones) for that key.

- Steer your brain away from linear thinking, "next note, next note," and visualize pitches that are important to the phrase while playing.

# Kaleidoscopic Learning

A stand-alone riff or melodic extract contains a series of relationships—as does an entire piece of music. When you learn to identify those features and maintain the interrelationships across a number of keys you are then able to:

⬧ Perceive pivotal melodic and rhythmic ingredients in a musical phrase.

⬧ Prepare for any eventuality that might come up when you learn a new composition.

## WHAT IS A KALEI?

A **Kalei** (denoted by the letter "K" and pronounced "Kuh-lie"), is a "Julie-ism" derived from the word "kaleidoscopic." I use the term *Kalei* to describe a mental perspective you can choose to adopt as a learning tactic to any musical phrase.

Let's use this riff to demonstrate four common Kaleis you can apply to help define any riff you move through the twelve keys.

### K 1

Identify the interval between each two notes. For instance, this example opens with a jump up of an octave, followed by a minor sixth down. The more skilled you become with your basic intervals, the faster you will recognize this Kalei in each musical phrase.

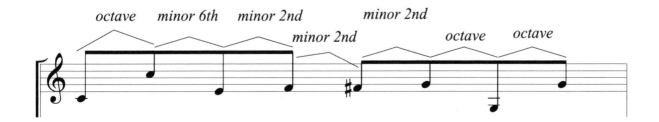

## K2

View the phrase in relationship to the scale and arpeggio for the key. In this case, it's more useful to locate the one note that isn't in the arpeggio (root, third, and fifth) or scale.

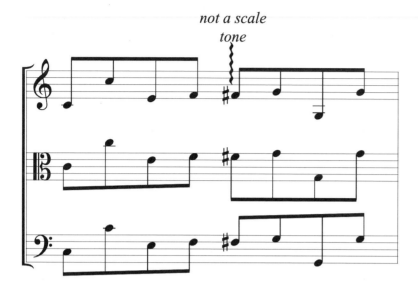

## K3

Identify the notes in the phrase by using numbers. As you'll see in the example below, the raised fourth is a lead tone into the fifth, but it can also be identified as a flatted fifth. Particularly in blues and jazz.

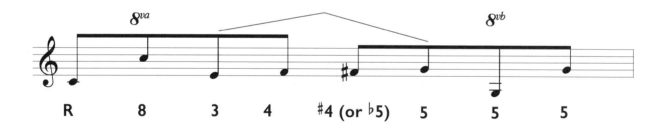

*Note:* When written using integers without music notation, you can apply an underline or boldface to indicate any pitch that moves under the root of the key.

## K4

In addition to identifying the intervals between the pitches as defined above in **K1**, you can also practice identifying those intervals as **whole** (W) and **half** (h) steps.

Refer to the *Interval Chart* in the chapter, "Interval Practice," for a comprehensive overview of the intervals.

# How to Work with Twelve Keys

# What are the Twelve Keys?

Though some keys have two names with notes that are identified by either sharps or flats, the pitches themselves sound out as the same. For instance, a C♯ and a D♭ are basically the same pitch. Below is a list of all the possible keys.

**Key of C**

**Key of D♭ or C♯**

**Key of D**

**Key of E♭ or D♯**

**Key of E**

**Key of F**

**Key of G♭ or F♯**

**Key of G**

**Key of A♭ or G♯**

**Key of A**

**Key of B♭ or A♯**

**Key of B or C♭**

"Enharmonic," refers to two notes that bear different names but are the same pitch, like F sharp and G flat.

## How Do I Choose Between Two Enharmonic Keys?

The Twelve-Key Approach encourages you to choose whichever key is easier for you to think in… to begin with. Later, if desired, you can also work on its enharmonic counterpart. For instance, the key of B♭ has two flats, whereas its enharmonic counterpart, A♯, has ten sharps! Only the keys of G♭ and F♯ meet as equals: six flats versus six sharps.

# Should I Learn Key Signatures?

Each exercise, riff, or musical phrase in this book can be learned and moved through the twelve keys without knowledge of the key signatures. This can be accomplished by paying attention to relationships between neighboring pitches as you audiate (hear) the line in your inner ear. In this case, you will have activated your right brain, which tracks maps and spatial relationships; your auditory system, located in the temporal lobe; and muscle memory, located in your motor cortices found on the right and left sides of the brain.

To activate your left brain, you must also apply analytical facilities while practicing. This can require cold memorization of the name of the keys, number of sharps or flats, and their names. Or, you can use the circle of fifths. **The twelve-key approach advocates knowledge through process rather than memorization.** If you forget information, you will then have a guaranteed process to apply that simultaneously enriches the maps you'll need to play well.

## THE CIRCLE OF FIFTHS

Any of the exercises in this book can be circled down in fifths to make your way through the twelve keys. This motion, called *cycling*, will also help you learn your key signatures in the flat keys. If this is new to you, count up four steps to find the key that will fall a fifth below. For instance, **C (1) » D (2) » E (3) » F (4)**. Or count down five steps: **C (1) » B (2) » A (3) » G (4) » F (5)**. Notice how, each time you descend a fifth, you find a key that picks up one flat in its key signature. Here's a handy way to remember this:

To go **FLAT** is to move down. Cycle **DOWN** in fifths to find your flat keys!

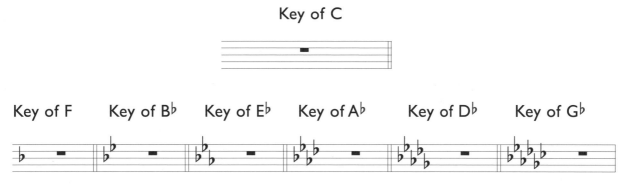

Conversely, to go **SHARP** is to move up. Cycle **UP** in fifths to find your sharp keys!

C (1) » D (2) » E (3) » F (4) » **G (5)**. Or down in fourths. C » B » A » **G (4)**

# How To Move Through the Keys

There are at least four major systems you can employ to move through the twelve keys. It's well worth exploring all of the following approaches. You might wonder, "Why bother?" Or, "Why not move through the twelve keys the same way every time?" Keep one important point in mind: As soon as you feel comfortable, it's time to deepen the challenge. Never let muscle memory take over completely. Maintain awareness and direction from your mind.

This practice system is guided by these three precepts:

◇ If you're comfortable enough to daydream, it's time to change your practice regimen.

◇ If muscle memory takes over and you have no idea what you're playing, it's time to rest and return when able to fully focus.

◇ If one skill eclipses all others, shift to a weaker skill. Eventually, you'll be able to shift mental "muscles" at will and a new mindful interaction will gradually replace your old mental habits.

> Never let your brain go to sleep. Hear, visualize, name before you sound out each note. Use note names that generate a clear mental picture and therefore make it easier for you to play accurately.

## FOUR TYPES OF 12-KEY MOTION

### Cycle Down in Fifths

As mentioned earlier, you can move through the twelve keys by moving down in fifths. When you reach the tipping point, i.e. you've reached the end of the range of your instrument, move up a fourth. For instance, a fifth down from the key of C is the key of F. If your instrument doesn't have an F available below your lowest C, you will find an F four steps above the C.

*Note: The following examples use enharmonic note names. Feel free to make any changes needed. For instance, if it's easier for you to visualize and play in the key of Gb versus F#, then that's the way to go.*

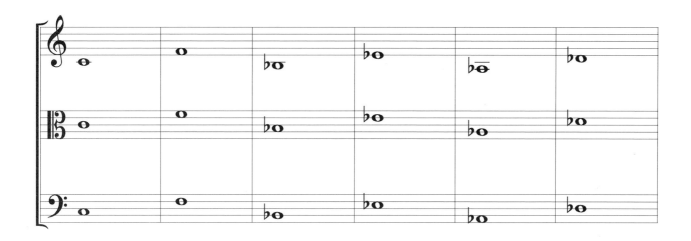

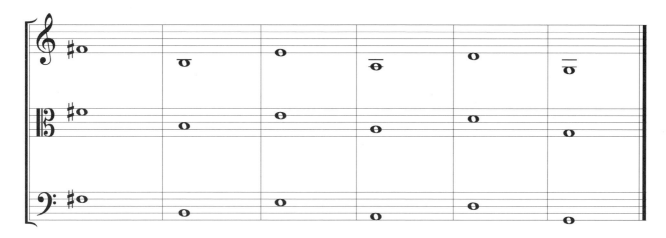

## Chromatic Motion: Ascending and Descending

It's possible to journey through the twelve keys by moving up or down in half steps. This is called *chromatic motion*. Assign note names according to comfort.

## Whole Tone Motion: Ascending and Descending

When you move through the keys using whole steps, you will return to the pitch you started on after you cover the first six keys. To cover the other six keys, you can either move up or down a half step. Again, assign sharp or flat names according to comfort.

## Diminished Motion: Ascending and Descending

Similarly, when you move through the keys using minor thirds, you will return to the pitch you started on after you cover the first four keys. To cover the next four keys, you can either move up or down a half step. Repeat this process to cover the final four keys.

# Directional Practice Techniques

# What is a DPT?

A *Directional Practice Technique* (DPT) refers to any practice technique you use to master a scale, musical phrase or piece of music. The idea behind any DPT, is to challenge your ability to maintain a clear mental picture of the notes you wish to master. We will focus on scale practice in this chapter. In particular, the addition of an interval above or below a scale tone. See the chapter, "The Path to Mastery," for fifty scale options.

You can choose any interval from the *Interval Chart* on the next page and practice partnering that interval with each note of a scale of your choice. The scale can be chromatic, a scale consisting solely of half steps, or diatonic. A Western diatonic scale combines half and whole steps. The order of those half and whole steps will define the type of scale. For instance, a major scale moves as follows: **Whole » W » half » W » W » W » h**

It is far easier to apply an interval to a chromatic (half step) scale to get started. This is because, if you choose a diatonic scale for your Directional Practice session, you will not be able to maintain consistent space between the scale tone and the chosen interval. In order to stay true to the notes of the scale, the interval will have to fluctuate by a half step. For instance, using the example of thirds, if you play a C major scale and place a third above each note of the scale, some thirds will be major (M3) and some will be minor (m3) unless you want to play notes outside of the scale tones.

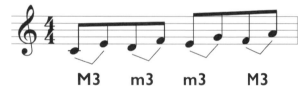

**M3    m3    m3    M3**

By contrast, here's an example using consistent major thirds placed over a chromatic scale. This practice is just as useful because you will gain the ability to move seamlessly through the notes of chromatic scale.

---

*Note: The following examples in this chapter are not notated across a full octave because it might be too tempting to play what you read, rather than apply Trilateral Learning:* **audiate, visualize, and analyze**.

---

# INTERVAL CHART

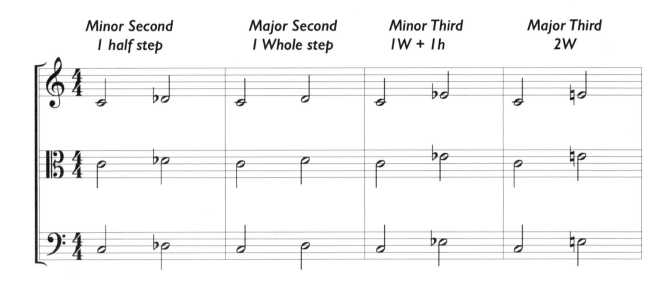

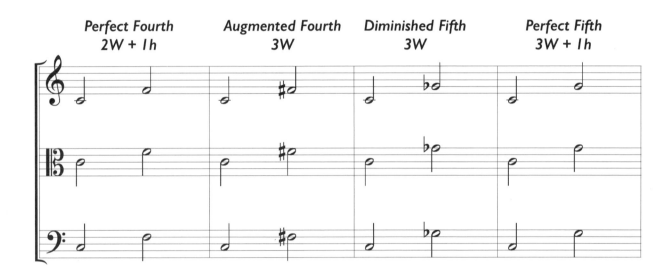

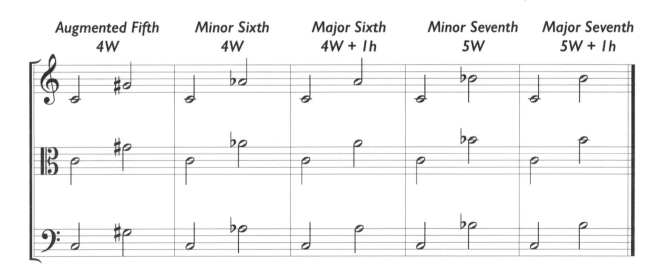

When applying any DPT to your practice sessions, start with one octave up and back down in all twelve keys. As ready, add a second and even a third octave if possible.

## FOUR APPROACHES TO INTERVAL PRACTICE

There are four possible ways you can practice the notes of a scale when coupled with the interval of your choice. In the following four examples, we will use a chromatic (half step) scale coupled with a major third.

We will discuss other options in depth later in this chapter.

### Bottoms Up

In this example, the scale tone can be found on the bottom and the interval has been placed above the scale tone.

### Tops Down

Notice how we still couple a major third with the notes of a chromatic scale, but now you will play the top note first (the major third above each chromatic scale tone) before following it with a note from the scale. This requires *Duplex Thinking*, a Julie-ism for holding two notes simultaneously in your right brain's mapping system. In this case, you must continue to hear and picture the notes of the chromatic scale, picture the third above, play it first, then descend to the scale tone.

> Remember... once you master a practice technique, it's time to move on to the next challenge!

Earlier in the book, we discussed the benefits of practice with mindful participation rather than half-awake habitual repetition. It won't take long for the practice techniques above to become instilled into your motor cortices. Your brain will want to go to sleep and let your muscle memory take over. That's when it's time to heighten the challenge. Either choose a different key, a new type of scale, a different interval, or try the following:

## Alternate Directions: Bottoms Up Alternated with Tops Down

In this next example, an ascending third is followed by a descending third. This requires an even stronger mental map. You must constantly picture the notes of the scale regardless of which pitches you play. The mental calisthenics will help flip you out of linear, sequential thinking, "next note, next note," into holding a dimensional picture of a number of pitches simultaneously. Keyboard players and guitarists do this all the time, but if you play a melody instrument, this might be fatiguing at first until your brain literally grows the cells required to handle the load. This first example is built on the notes of a C major scale. Therefore, as discussed earlier, the intervals will fluctuate between major and minor thirds.

Here's the same practice technique as applied to major thirds built on a chromatic scale:

## *Alternate Directions: Tops Down Alternated with Bottoms Up*

You can also reverse the order.

# COMPOUND DPTs

Try combining two intervals to deepen the challenge. This particular combination consists of two stacked major thirds—two major thirds in succession. It also mirrors the arpeggio of an augmented chord: root, major third, sharp five. The bottom note for each stack moves up chromatically.

## *Bottoms Up*

## Tops Down

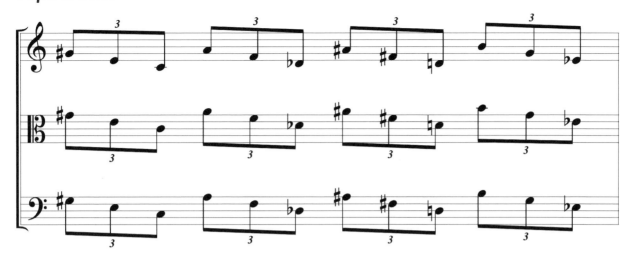

## Bottoms Up, Tops Down

## Tops Down, Bottoms Up

Any compound DPT can be constructed of like on top of like—as you've seen in the previous examples—or you can mix intervals, as is demonstrated next. This pattern consists of a whole step followed by a perfect fourth. If you aren't familiar with perfect fourths, you might want to practice applying that interval to each note of a chromatic scale first and then combine the two intervals. See the *Interval Chart* on page 31 for assistance.

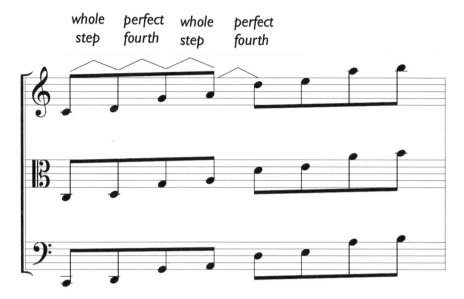

## RHYTHMIC VARIATIONS

It's always useful to start with a consistent rhythm, like quarter or eighth notes. But you can deepen the challenge by adding rhythmic variations. The possibilities are endless.

**Example One.**

The following example looks simple, doesn't it? Two sixteenth notes followed by three eighth notes.

However, if we combine that rhythmic figure with our three-note stacked major thirds—bottoms up alternated with tops down—the rhythmic phrase will gradually shift across our three-note figure: I » 3 » #5 // #5 » 3 » 1

*Note: Always stabilize a new exercise before moving it through the twelve keys.*

The idea behind any DPT you spotlight during practice is to heighten the challenge, so the more variables you add, the more you'll test the strength of your map of the notes. You can adorn any melodic figure with repetitions, articulations, accidentals, or any other ornamentation you would like to apply.

## Example Two.

It's amazing how quickly you can transform drab scale-work into really interesting and fun practice by replacing traditionally symmetrical rhythms, like quarter or eighth notes, with more complex rhythmic phrasing. The example shown below is built on a major pentatonic scale. If you aren't familiar with this scale, first use straight quarter notes to play it up and down through the twelve keys: **R 2 3 5 6 8**

Next, apply the following rhythmic figure. This example moves chromatically, but how you move the phrase through the twelve keys is entirely up to you.

Let's build on this idea by lengthening it to four beats and capping it with a flatted third, a notes that's outside the major pentatonic scale. This introduces a bluesy twist to the idea.

Let's add a measure to create a question and answer feel to this musical idea. Notice how the rhythmic shape generates a question and answer feel:

If we combine notes from the minor pentatonic scale, we can expand our initial phrase even further.

**1 ♭3 4 5 ♭7**

Try moving this iteration through the twelve keys using the numbering system to get your noggin cranking! To indicate the fact that the flatted third is positioned above the octave, that degree of the scale has been numbered accordingly with a " ♭10."

[8 = octave; 9 = second degree above the octave; ♭10 = the third degree above the octave]

**R 2 3 5 6 ♭10 8**

**R 2 3 5 6 ♭10 8 ♭7**

Move the full phrase through the twelve keys.

# Interval Practice

## WHY IS IT IMPORTANT TO MASTER THE BASIC INTERVALS?

In the earlier chapter, "The Twelve Key Approach," we defined Kaleis as perceptual tools designed to help you navigate. A command over intervals will enhance this process. If you are a reading musician, you've hopefully developed the ability to hear what you see as you automatically translate symbols on a page into muscle moves. What if you could also immediately perceive and hear the interrelationships between pitches in every phrase? Interval practice will help you achieve that goal.

> All intervals are made up of half and whole steps.

## PRACTICE TECHNIQUES

During practice, choose an interval from the Interval Chart on page 31 and apply it to a chromatic scale to cover the twelve keys. Try to hear each couplet before you play it. Apply the Directional Practice techniques we covered earlier and, when ready, compound figures—a combination of two or more intervals applied consistently to each note of the chromatic scale.

You might want to start out by singing the intervals. It's helpful to use a drone accompaniment. If you don't have the software to generate a drone, try using the recording, *Cello Drones* by Navarro Music. Can't hear certain intervals? Find a popular melody that features that interval or walk up using a scale or intervals that are more familiar. For instance, let's say you can't hear a perfect fourth, but a fifth comes naturally. Sing up a fifth and down a whole step. Or move to a major third, then up a half step. The key is to use what you already know to support learning the less familiar.

> Use the scales, intervals or popular melodies you're already familiar with to teach yourself the intervals you have difficulty hearing.

## Interval Practice Examples

You have already practiced and will practice minor seconds every time you apply a chosen interval to the chromatic scale, which is made up of all half steps. So these first four examples demonstrate *Directional Practice Techniques* as applied to the major second.

Practice each interval exercise across an octave and back or, even more useful, from the bottom two notes on your instrument sequentially up to the top two notes—within reason—and back again. This provides an opportunity to isolate and master that targeted interval across the full range of your instrument, and to work out fingering choices based on two criteria:

- Know where you are at all times. It might be tempting to play by ear but you will get far more out of this exercise by tracking the notes and degrees of each key you are in.

- Take a moment to think beyond this exercise to the most useful fingering system you can apply. If you only focus on each exercise as a one-time pursuit, you might miss out on its potential. Try to imagine all the contexts this particular motion across your instrument might appear in, and make decisions that will serve future challenges and scenarios.

The one-measure examples that follow are only meant to demonstrate the application of each interval to the chromatic scale. As with other exercises in this book, they have not been notated in full to challenge you to flip the mental switch out of a "follow the leader" mind-set to ownership over every key and type of scale. The emphasis should be on picturing the interval, naming the notes, hearing each partner note in relation to the base notes of the chromatic scale, and making fingering choices that will best serve your future needs.

> Visualize, hear and name the interval you place above every note of the chromatic scale before you sound it out.

**Note:** *The exercises in this chapter have been designed to get you started. Moving forward, you can choose any single interval to focus on or combine two or three to deepen the challenge.*

## MAJOR SECONDS, BOTTOMS UP

## MAJOR SECONDS, TOPS DOWN

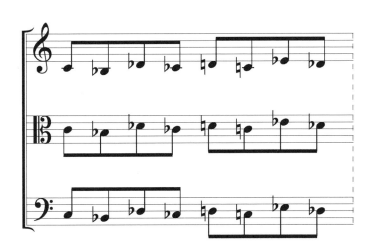

## MAJOR SECONDS, BOTTOMS UP...TOPS DOWN

## MAJOR SECONDS, TOPS DOWN... BOTTOMS UP

As with the major second exercises, apply the following to each of these intervals through the twelve keys. Use the scale of your choice. See *Fifty World Maps* in "The Path to Mastery."

- ◇ Bottoms Up
- ◇ Tops Down
- ◇ Bottoms Up, Tops Down
- ◇ Tops Down, Bottoms up

## MINOR THIRDS

## MAJOR THIRDS

## PERFECT FOURTHS

## DIMINISHED FIFTHS

## PERFECT FIFTHS

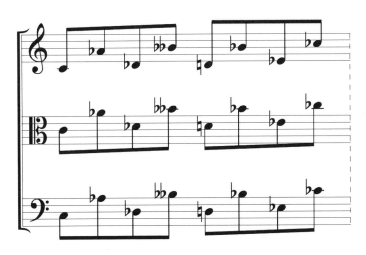

## MINOR SIXTHS

## MAJOR SIXTHS

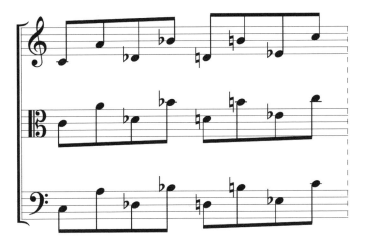

## MINOR SEVENTHS

## MAJOR SEVENTHS

When we alternate between two or more intervals to create a compound figure, we can use enharmonic names for our notes. How do we decide how to name and notate each pitch? Base it on whatever is clearest to you as a player.

# Compound Figures ♭♭♯

Any interval can be combined two ways and applied to all twelve keys:

- First interval followed by second interval (in this case, a major second followed by a major third).

- Second interval followed by first interval (in this case, a major third followed by a major second).

## MAJOR SECOND ALTERNATED WITH MAJOR THIRD

This is a different paradigm. We no longer need to adhere to a key signature as our guide. We are maneuvering through a crystal-like structure that provides its own internal guidelines. Thus, note names can be determined via whatever identity is clearer or easier to find on your instrument. Notice how this next example combines sharps and flats. In the opening, the F♯ and A♯ in the second beat could just as easily be thought of as a G♭ to a B♭.

## MAJOR THIRD ALTERNATED WITH MAJOR SECOND

## THREE INTERVALS

What happens when we combine three intervals, like a major second, minor third, and a major third? We end up with six possible combinations.

◇ **Minor third (m3) » major second (M2) » major third (M3).**

◇ **m3 » M3 » M2**

◇ **M2 » M3 » m3**

◇ **M2 » m3 » M3**

◇ **M3 » m3 » M2**

◇ **M3 » M2 » m3**

We can also exponentially increase our practice material if, instead of stacking straight upwards from each note in a chromatic scale as demonstrated earlier in this chapter, we make a zig-zag pattern by stepping back a note and then skipping to the next interval.

What's the point? Each time you trick your body's first instinct, which is to rely on a combination of muscle and auditory memory, you increase your level of mastery. Using this approach, you will challenge your right brain to create a detailed map of all possibilities in every key by building a dimensional road-map. We're doing everything possible to steer away from traditionally popular linear, sequential key practice that has been overstimulated by scale-work, so we keep heightening the challenge to hold onto every detail of that map. If you lose where you are, no worries. Step back to work with one interval, then add a second and then a third. You will build mental stamina and each map will eventually become second nature.

Look at the lines added to this zigzag version of the previous example. The marked notes follow the alternating pattern of a major second, with a major third, followed by a minor third. Each tagged note has a partner note it moves down to which also follows the same sequence. This exercise will force you to visualize two completely different tracks simultaneously.

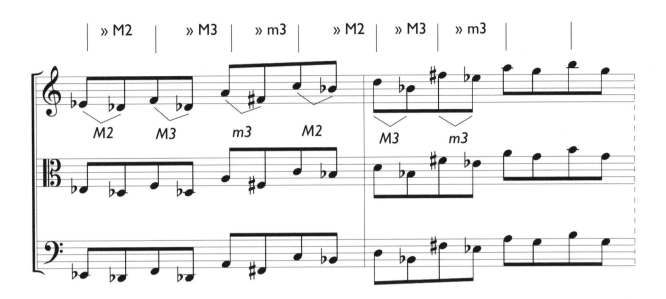

There are some physical exercises at the gym that members don't like. They do them anyway, because they know those exercises will balance their strength or flexibility. Other activities are beneficial and enjoyable. It's all personal. One person's treasure is another person's nemesis. This will likely be the case with these combinations.

In fact, some sequences may not yield a sound that interests you at all, while you may opt to incorporate other patterns into compositions or improvisations. For instance, here's a personal favorite: a descending whole step that moves up a perfect fourth:

## WHOLE STEP DOWN ALTERNATED WITH PERFECT FOURTH UP

# Learning a Melody 12-Key Style

The brain is like a beehive. It stores each nugget of information in its own, sequestered cell. A new context can fool your brain into thinking you are learning something different, even if that isn't the case… until you mindfully connect the dots by literally teaching your brain to synapse—create a junction—between two chambers.

You can practice a melody for hours, days, weeks and months but that doesn't necessarily mean you will gain full use of the colorful gems embedded in its substrata.

Here's another practice technique to add to your vocabulary. We're going to apply these steps to the traditional Irish melody, "Danny Boy" to walk you through the process.

⬦ Scan the piece for repetitious melodic excerpts, including transposed lines.

⬦ Tap the rhythms or play them on a single pitch.

⬦ Familiarize yourself with the melodic landscape by playing the piece a few times.

⬦ Analyze the piece phrase-by-phrase for interval motion by penciling in the degree over each note as well as the distance between each couplet.

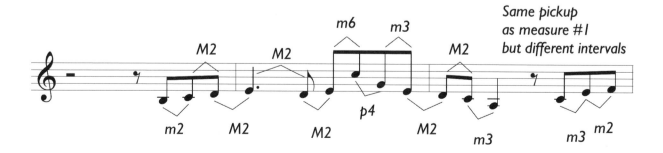

7 1 2   3   2 3 8 5 3   2 1 6   1 3 4   5   6 5 3 1 3   2

- ◇ Focus on the first phrase and move it through the twelve keys. Try not to do this by ear. Track the interval relationships to transpose it.

- ◇ Move to the second phrase. Scan it for interval content and take note of any motion that mirrors the first phrase. Continue with the third phrase.

- ◇ Notice the start and end notes for each of the three phrases and move them through twelve keys. Here's an example of a hybrid of these phrases.

Yes, this is a lot of work!

But you will only need to process a few melodies like this before the vista opens up. Then you can apply these steps to phrases that are outside your wheelhouse. You'll also begin to notice these relationships automatically each time you work on a new piece.

Each time you trick your body's first instinct, which is to rely on a combination of muscle and auditory memory, you increase your level of mastery.

# Three-Part Chords ♭♭♯

## MAJOR:
## I » 3 » 5

(CM, CMaj., CΔ)

## MINOR:
## I » ♭3 » 5

(Cm, Cmin., C-)

## DIMINISHED:
## I » ♭3 » ♭5

(Cdim., C°)

## AUGMENTED:
## I » 3 » ♯5

(Caug., C+)

# WHY ARE CHORDS IMPORTANT?

When you understand the scaffold upon which each composer has built his or her composition—the chords—this will influence how you play. And of course, improvising musicians must be able to recognize and navigate across the harmonic motion chords generate.

If you've never worked with chords before, it's highly useful to learn the four basic three-part chords as a first step. Just as every tree has a trunk, every chord is built upon these.

> A three-part chord consists of the root, third, and fifth of the key. The type of third and fifth are determined by the chord symbol.

**Major:** 1 » 3 » 5

Symbols: Major, Maj., Δ

**Minor:** 1 » ♭3 » 5

Symbols: min., m, -

**Diminished:** 1 » ♭3 » ♭5

Symbols: dim., o

**Augmented:** 1 » 3 » ♯5

Symbols: aug., +

## Practice Techniques

To learn your chords, the most common practice is through cold memorization of the facts, i.e., a diminished chord is defined as root, flatted third and flatted fifth. This locks the information into your mind. But we also need to instill the chords into your ears, right-brain map, and physical technique. We will focus on this more comprehensive approach to learning chords on your instrument. Therefore, this process has been designed to provide you with access to all the chord tones everywhere on your instrument simultaneously as follows:

◇ Play the root, third, and fifth of each of the four chords in all twelve keys across one octave.

◇ Play the chord tones across two, then three octaves, if possible.

◇ Apply all six permutations outlined on the next page to each of the four chords across the twelve keys.

**Note:** *If you faithfully apply **Trilateral Learning**—hear/name/visualize each note before you play it—you will boost your musicianship considerably since almost all melodies are built on minor and major thirds in one way or another.*

## CHORD TONE PERMUTATIONS FOR THREE-PART CHORDS

Remember *Kaleidoscopic Layering*, the art of perceiving and practicing the same material from as many vantage points as possible? Rather than the standard approach to chord tones, root followed by the third and then the fifth, we will apply permutations to chord tone practice. I introduced the term *permutations* in the opening material to describe this practice approach.

1.  1 » 3 » 5

2.  1 » 5 » 3

3.  3 » 5 » 1

4.  3 » 1 » 5

5.  5 » 1 » 3

6.  5 » 3 » 1

Apply these six permutations to each of the four three-part chords across all twelve keys. Then circle back and repeat in the upper octave.

## SCALE TONE PRACTICE

There is a prescribed scale for each type of chord. It's called a *chordal scale*. When we hear or see the word "scale," we immediately picture playing the tonic—the root of the key—followed by sequential pitches up to the octave and back. This approach to practice yields only a percentage of all that's potentially available to you. Music doesn't consist of scales running up and down, up and down. Excellent musicianship requires the ability to perceive any and all schematics within a family of pitches across the entire accessible range of your instrument.

Try thinking of a scale as a map that has no beginning or end: Each note exists with equal presence on your instrument, waiting patiently for its turn to sing!

You can practice mini-fragments of the chordal scales by applying DPTs. On the following page, you'll find a sample pattern in groups of three.

This approach to practice will enable you to develop a more realistic skill-set to be able to flexibly dance across the chord and scale tones on your instrument. For instance, you will be able to start on any given chord tone in any of the twelve keys and walk down (or up) through neighboring scale tones to the next chord tone. This will require a clear mental picture of the yellow brick road—the chord tones—in each key, as well as half and whole step motion as dictated by the chord's symbol.

Let's apply this practice approach to the chordal scales for each of the four chords.

**Note:** *In many of the twelve keys, there will be moments when you'll need to decide between a correctly named note and an enharmonically named note. And you may even name it differently a moment later within a new context as shown below. For instance, the following example has replaced the double-flatted seventh—the double-flatted B—with an A. The C flat has been replaced with a B. As you practice the diminished scale and three-part chords across the twelve keys, feel free to choose enharmonic note names that support fluidity and clarity.*

## SCALE BUILT FROM THE MAJOR CHORD:

1 » 2 » 3 » 4 » 5 » 6 » 7 » 8

## EXERCISE BUILT ON THE MAJOR CHORDAL SCALE

3 2 1 » 5 4 3 » 7 6 5 » 10 9 8 » 5 6 7 » 3 4 5 » 1 2 3 » 1

## SCALE BUILT FROM THE C MINOR CHORD

1 » 2 » b3 » 4 » 5 » 6 » b7 » 8

## EXERCISE BUILT ON THE MINOR CHORDAL SCALE

b3 2 1 » 5 4 b3 » b7 6 5 » b10 9 8 » 5 6 b7 » b3 4 5 » 1 2 b3 » 1

## SCALE BUILT FROM THE C DIMINISHED CHORD

1 » 2 » b3 » 4 » b5 » b6 » bb7 (same as a 6) » 7

# EXERCISE BUILT ON THE DIMINISHED CHORDAL SCALE

The diminished scale is unique. Built on a whole step/half step pattern, it's far more useful to only focus on the motion of minor thirds for its chord tones. Each scale tone will fall one whole step above each chord tone. This scale truly requires you to create a mental map of the minor thirds that make up the chord tones, rather than thinking/picturing one note at a time, tonic to tonic. Enharmonic names are included in this example to assist you.

**Note:** *We are interested in strengthening your mental map of all the notes on your instrument. For an extra challenge, apply these chordal scale exercises from the lowest point to the highest—within reason—on your instrument and back again. In this case, you will not be moving tonic to tonic so your ears will not be able to take over as easily. Depending on the range of your instrument, you might be starting on the third, the fifth, or the seventh of the key rather than walking from the third to the root.*

When you enter diminished territory, choose note names that provide you with clarity... even if it means changing the name of the same pitch a beat or two later.

## SCALE BUILT FROM THE C AUGMENTED CHORD

The augmented scale is also called a whole-tone scale. Each note is a whole step apart. Without half steps in the scale, there are only six notes rather than the traditional seven.

---

## EXERCISE BUILT ON THE SCALE FROM THE AUGMENTED CHORD

There is another chord that shares the same chord tones but offers a more contemporary version of the scale. It's called half-diminished half-augmented scale, also referred to in jazz circles as the altered or alt scale. You will find this chord listed in the *Four-Part Chords* section in a few pages. The altered scale's chord symbol looks like this: +7♭9

# Four-Part Chords

The base of each of the following four-part chords contains the same pitches as outlined in the three-part chord section. Four-part chords include either the sixth or the seventh on top. There are nine chords that are useful to learn. Some of them share the same scales we just covered, while others offer more complex scales. The work you've done to master the three-part chords will enable you to learn these chords more quickly.

Traditionally, instrumentalists have practiced chord tones by applying inversions. Here's an example using the notes of a C major chord:

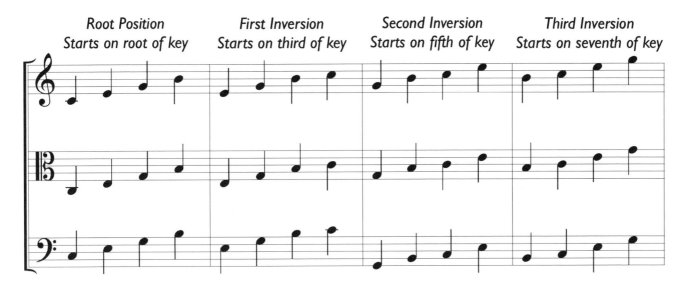

| Root Position | First Inversion | Second Inversion | Third Inversion |
|---|---|---|---|
| Starts on root of key | Starts on third of key | Starts on fifth of key | Starts on seventh of key |

The additional fourth note increases the number of permutations possible during practice from six combinations of the notes in any given chord to twenty-four. When you apply these twenty-four permutations to each of the nine four-part chords across all twelve keys, this requires the zenith of mental mapping. You can also circle back and add an octave or two. It's a bit like participating in a triathlon!

How do you remember the permutations you've already covered? Feel free to come up with a solution other than the one presented here. The solution offered in *Twelve-Key Practice* offers every possible permutation that starts on the root of the chord. Then I've coupled the root with the fifth, then the root with the seventh before moving to the series that start on the third of the key.

When you apply twenty-four permutations to nine chords in one key, you're looking at 216 possible combinations of the chord tones. Applied to twelve keys? 2,592 possible combinations!

Given the depth of practice involved here, one key a day or one key a week or even one key a month will yield enormous results. Particularly since our goal is to visualize, hear, and name before playing each note.

But hey! Here's yet another way to approach practice. Choose **ONE** permutation and apply it to **ONE** type of chord. Then repeat this procedure through the twelve keys.

# NINE FOUR-PART CHORDS

## MAJOR SEVENTH

1 » 3 » 5 » 7

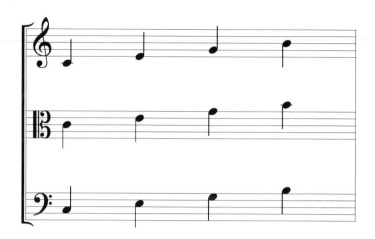

## DOMINANT SEVENTH

1 » 3 » 5 » ♭7

## MAJOR SIXTH

1 » 3 » 5 » 6

# MINOR
## SEVENTH

1 » ♭3 » 5 » ♭7

# MINOR SIXTH

1 » ♭3 » 5 » 6

# DIMINISHED

1 » ♭3 » ♭5 » ♭♭7

## AUGMENTED

1 » 3 » #5 » b7

## MINOR/MAJOR

1 » b3 » 5 » 7

## ALTERED

1 » 3 » #5 » b7

# 24 Chord-Tone Permutations for Four-Part Chords

These permutations can be applied to any of the nine chord types illustrated on the previous pages.

| | |
|---|---|
| 1 » 3 » 5 » 7 | 3 » 5 » 7 » 1 |
| 1 » 3 » 7 » 5 | 3 » 5 » 1 » 7 |
| 1 » 5 » 3 » 7 | 3 » 7 » 1 » 5 |
| 1 » 5 » 7 » 3 | 3 » 7 » 5 » 1 |
| 1 » 7 » 3 » 5 | 3 » 1 » 5 » 7 |
| 1 » 7 » 5 » 3 | 3 » 1 » 7 » 5 |
| 5 » 7 » 1 » 3 | 7 » 1 » 3 » 5 |
| 5 » 7 » 3 » 1 | 7 » 1 » 5 » 3 |
| 5 » 1 » 3 » 7 | 7 » 3 » 5 » 1 |
| 5 » 1 » 7 » 3 | 7 » 3 » 1 » 5 |
| 5 » 3 » 1 » 7 | 7 » 5 » 1 » 3 |
| 5 » 3 » 7 » 1 | 7 » 5 » 3 » 1 |

# The Golden Chord ♭♭♯

Back in the early 1980's, I sat down on my New York City music studio's floor and surrounded myself with every fake book I owned (these are back-street blues/jazz repertoire books). I closed my eyes and randomly opened each book to a blues, swing or jazz tune. Some tunes were from the 1930s and some were contemporary, depending on the book. Pencil in hand, I made a note of the number of major, minor, diminished, augmented, and dominant seventh chords I found in each tune. The results were the same. Each tune had far more dominant seventh chords than any other chord in it. In fact, in some cases, up to seventy-five percent. "Aha," I thought. This is the chord I'll focus on when I practice.

> The dominant seventh chord is made up of a major third, perfect fifth, and flatted seventh. It is an extremely popular chord, found in church music as well as folk, blues, swing, jazz, Latin, and pop styles. It's the GOLDEN CHORD!

**The dominant seventh chord has a job.** Think of it as a Pied Piper. Its sound tells us we need to be on the move, that it's time to go home, i.e. **down a fifth**. Compare that to the job of the major chord. Its sound tells us that we've arrived and may not want to travel anyplace new after that!

If you picture or play a C major scale and imagine building chords from every degree of its scale, you will find the dominant seventh on the fifth degree of the scale: R 3 5 ♭7

Since the dominant seventh chord—also referred to as the seventh chord—leads us down a fifth, it's not surprising that when you look through tune books, you can predict the chord that will follow any seventh chord. The dominant seventh chord will almost always lead you down a fifth to the next chord.

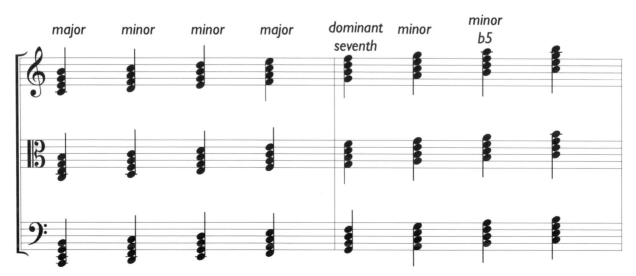

> The dominant seventh chord will almost always lead you down a fifth to the next chord. This is called "cycling."

The exercises in this section of the book are quite extensive. My reasoning is as follows:

- ◇ Once you learn the major third of every key, it's easy to flat it as needed.

- ◇ Once you learn the perfect fifth of every key, it's easy to flat or sharp it as needed.

- ◇ Once you learn the flatted seventh of every key, it's easy to raise it a half step.

When you focus on the most popular chord in all styles of music—the dominant seventh chord—and are able to easily play the permutations on the following pages in all twelve keys, you will have boosted your technique and musicianship to new heights.

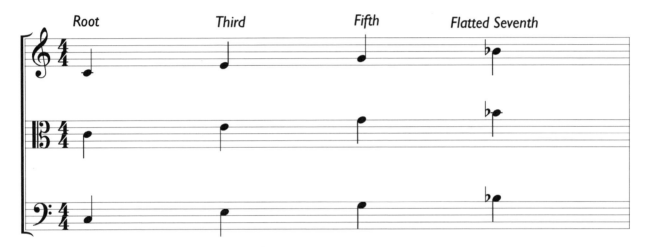

> The chordal scale that's built on the dominant seventh is a major scale with a flatted seventh. This is the same scale we use for one of the seven modes, the Mixolydian mode.

Focus on each step until fully mastered throughout the twelve keys before you move forward to the next step and the next. The criteria you can apply for moving from exercise to exercise is as follows (this will sound familiar):

- ◇ Can I hear the next pitch before I play it?

- ◇ Can I visualize the next pitch before I physically play it?

- ◇ Can I name the note and the degree of the scale before I play it?

- ◇ Can I apply all three of these steps throughout the twelve keys?

# Thirty-Five Cycle Exercises

*Note: Just a reminder…* *If you reach the bottom of your instrument's range, you will need to find your next start note an octave higher to cycle down a fifth. A fifth below the present key is the same as a fourth above. For instance, the key of F is a fifth below the key of C. If you count from C up through its scale tones, you'll find F is the fourth degree of the scale.*

## 1) CYCLE DOWN THROUGH THE ROOT NOTES OF ALL 12 KEYS

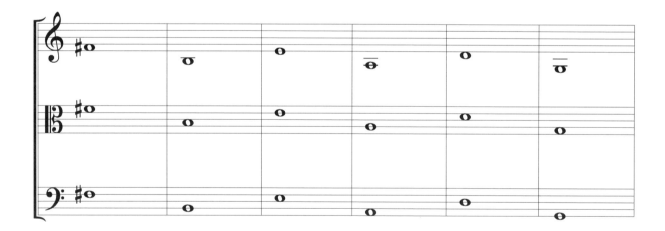

"Cycle," or "move through the cycle" are both terms that refer to a motion downward the distance of a fifth, or up a fourth, through the twelve keys.

It might seem counterintuitive to start out only playing the root and third of each key. After all, why not just start with all four chord tones: 1 » 3 » 5 » b7?

But each time you alter the exercise by one note, you challenge the map. Can you picture from the third of the present key to the root of the key that's found a fifth below? How about from the fifth of the present key to the root of the next key in the cycle?

**2)    1 » 3**

**3)    1 » 3 » 5**

**4)    1 » 3 » 5 » b7**

**5)   3 » 1**

**6)   5 » 3 » 1**

**7)   1 » 3 » ♭7 » 5 » 3 » 1**

## 8) TWO OCTAVES: 1 » 3 » 5 » ♭7

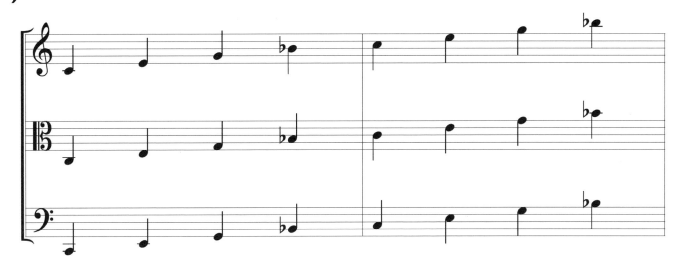

## 9) TWO OCTAVES: ♭7 » 5 » 3 » 1

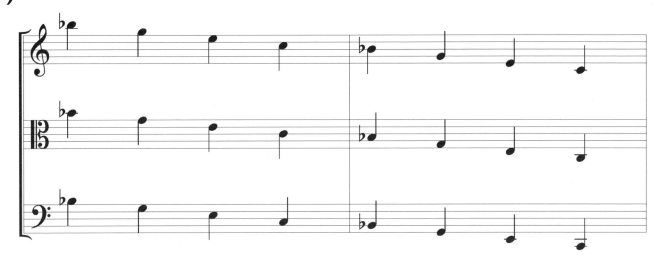

## 10) LOOPS 3 1 3 » 5 3 5 » ♭7 5 ♭7 » 8 ♭7 8

**11)**  ♭7  8  ♭7  » 5 ♭7  5  » 3  5  3  » 1

**12)**  First Inversion: 3  »  5  »  ♭7  »  1

**13)**  Second Inversion: 5  »  ♭7  »  1  »  3

## 14)    THIRD INVERSION: ♭7 » 1 » 3 » 5

## 15)    3 2 1 » 5 4 3 » ♭7 6 5 » 8

## 16)    8 9 10 » 5 6 ♭7 » 3 4 5 » 1

> You can always move any of these exercises into other octaves on your instrument.

## 17-24) GRACE NOTES

This next series of exercises consists of eight embellishments. As you practice applying each grace note, try to keep the emphasis light on the ornament itself with a legato transition to the core note.

There are a number of approaches to choose from for practice.

- ◇ Apply one ornament to the root notes of each key in the cycle.

- ◇ Apply all eight ornaments to the root note of each key.

- ◇ Apply one ornament to the root, third, fifth, and flatted seventh of each key.

- ◇ Apply all eight ornaments to the root, third, fifth, and flatted seventh of each key.

Depending on the instrument you play, you may need to occasionally use unusual fingerings to create a seamless motion between the ornament and chord tone.

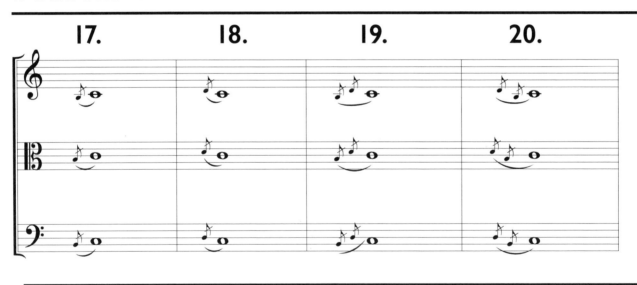

Remember to audiate, visualize, and name each note before you play it.

**25)**   R  »  4  »  5  »  ♭7

**26)**   1  »  3  »  #4  »  ♭7

**27)**   ♭7  »  #4  »  3  »  1

Remember *Kaleidoscopic Layering* and *Duplex Thinking*? Here's an opportunity to exercise a slightly different Kalei as you practice this last group of exercises: Try to visualize the root and octave in your mind's eye and ears while you play the other notes. Notice the interval relationships between the octave and each of those extensions: the ninth, eleventh, and sharp eleventh.

Ask yourself these questions as you play through the twelve keys:

⋄ Can I hear the ninth before I play it? Can I hear the sharp eleventh?

⋄ Can I picture how to play the note and name it before I play it?

⋄ Would I be able to play these notes "out of thin air" whenever I choose, in any context?

---

**28)**    I  » 3 » 5  » ♭7 » 9

---

**29)**    9 » ♭7 » 5 » 3 » I

**30)**   1  »  3  »  5  »  ♭7  »  9  »  #11

**31)**   #11  »  9  »  ♭7  »  5  »  3  »  1

**32)**   1  »  3  »  ♭5  »  ♭7

**33)**  ♭7  »  ♭5  »  3  »  1

**34)**  1 » 3 » ♭5 » ♭7 » 9

**35)**  1 » 3 » ♭5 » ♭7 » 9 » 11

# Riff Practice

Even though the term "riff" is generally used in pop and jazz, we'll use it to describe any succinct, catchy musical phrase. And all phrases are fair game. It can come from a tune or melody you're currently working on, an intriguing idea you lifted off someone else's solo, or your imagination. Since the intention is to push your skills to the next level, try to choose phrases that offer you the opportunity to increase your skills. Weak on finding the sixth of each key? Move a phrase that revolves around the sixth. Hear someone play something incredible? That's the one to learn.

> Riff: a short repeated phrase.

You can download audio from a Youtube video or choose a piece from iTunes and use software to slow it down. Some software will allow you to loop the phrase you want to learn. It can be extremely useful to sing along before you try to find the pattern of notes and rhythms on your instrument. Ears first, technique second.

It's also useful to learn musical phrases that were meant for another instrument. Often, an idea that's easy as pie on one instrument is difficult on another. It's also useful to learn ideas from a variety of styles of music. Scales and rhythms from other cultures will offer new treasures to work with.

**AUDITORY**

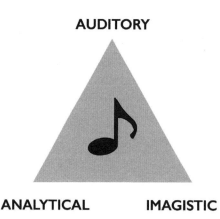

**ANALYTICAL**          **IMAGISTIC**

Don't forget to apply *Trilateral Learning* techniques and each of our four primary Kaleis.

## K1

Identify the intervals between each two notes of the phrase.

## K2

View the line in relationship to the scale and arpeggio for the key.

## K3

Identify the degrees of the notes in the phrase by identifying the degrees of the scale.

## K4

Practice identifying intervals as whole and half steps.

**Note:** *There is an advantage to learning the rhythmic phrase and the pitch sequence as separate steps before you combine them. It might take some getting used to, but try applying the rhythm to a single pitch before you reconnect it to the entire pitch sequence.*

# WHY THESE STYLES AND EXAMPLES?

Every region throughout the world has evolved a wealth of musical styles, each encapsulated in its own eco-system of rhythmic and pitch-to-pitch relationships. These examples were chosen in an attempt to present a cross-section of quintessential rhythmic and musical attributes and does not—nor can it possibly—represent the entire musical imagination of the world, or the entirety of a specific genre.

> If the riff is tricky, break it into pieces. Focus on one interval through the twelve keys or just a couple of beats. You don't have to practice segments in the order they appear. You can isolate any part of the riff.

# IMPORTANT NOTES

You might be tempted to rely on reading each riff rather than focusing on the conversion of each figure from degrees of the scale into a tonal map. That's why the standard notation for these examples has been placed at the back of this section.

- ◇ **The examples aren't alphabetized or in any hierarchical order.** The idea here isn't to move in a linear fashion through the phrases. Choose whichever phrase appeals to you.

- ◇ **The numbered degrees of the scale are not aligned with the rhythmic notation.** If you follow the suggested sequence below, the rhythmic phrase should be locked into your ears before you assign the pitches.

Follow this suggested sequence:

- ◇ Play the **RHYTHM** first.

- ◇ Assign **PITCHES** to the rhythms using the numbers provided.

- ◇ Isolate and master all tricky note-to-note motion within the phrase first.

- ◇ Refer to the chapter, *The Twelve-Key Approach* for details about cycling versus chromatic, diminished or whole tone navigation through the twelve keys.

# Classical Riffs

> **BOLD** = pitch can be found below the root.
> Brackets {5 5 5} = figure spans two beats.
> Arrows ( » ») separate beats.
> Backward double slash \\ separates measures.

There are, of course, thousands of examples to choose from within the classical repertoire. Hopefully, these examples will whet your appetite and inspire you to choose a phrase from your favorite composer and move it through the twelve keys.

### 1. Mozart

4 I » 4 I » 4 I 4 6 » 8

### 2. Bach

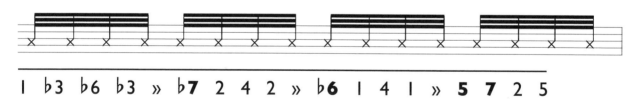

I ♭3 ♭6 ♭3 » ♭**7** 2 4 2 » ♭**6** I 4 I » **5 7** 2 5

### 3. Vivaldi

I \\ 3 3 3 » 2 I » 5

### 4. Beethoven

5 #4 \\ 5 #4 » 5 2 » ♮4 ♭3 » I

# American Roots Riffs

This is by no means a comprehensive list of styles, but there are enough here to integrate a taste of the musical imagination of the world into your twelve-key practice.

## 5. Appalachian Fiddle Tag

8 7 » 8 5 » 6 8 » 5 4 \\ 3 1 » 2 » 1

## 6. Cajun

5 1 » 3 4 3 » 2 1 » 7

## 7. Bluegrass

3 1 » b3 2 » 1 b7 » 5 b7 \\ 1

## 8. Western Swing

5 {1 » 1} » 5 6 5 4 \\ b3 5 4 b3 » 1

## 9. Franco-American

1 3 » 5 b7 » 9 » {8 \\ 8} » 5 » 3 5 » 9 » 8

# World Music Riffs

## 10. Irish

3 4 5 » 5 3 5 » b7 » 6 5 4 » 3 4 5 3 » 4 2 1

## 11. Scottish

**5** » I » 3 I » 5 I » 3 I

## 12. Klezmer

**5** I b3 5 » #4 5 b3 5 \\ #4 5 b3 5 » #4 b3 2 1

## 13. Cape Verde

I **7** I 2 » b3 4 » {5 5 5} \\ 5 4 b3 2 » I **7** » I

## 14. Afro-Cuban

I » 4 » b6 8 » 7 \\ 5 » 3 » {I » I}

Practice the rhythm on an open note. Slowly translate the degrees into pitches as half or quarter notes. Then combine pitch and rhythm and move through the twelve keys.

## 15. West African Kora

*Note: The West African riff spans two octaves and has been notated differently for clarity:*

Upper Octave, first two beats: 4  3  4  3  2  »  4  3  2  1  3  2  1  **7**
Lower Octave: 9  8  7  6  8  7  6  5  »  6  5  6  5  4  \\  3  5  {1 »1}

## 16. East Indian

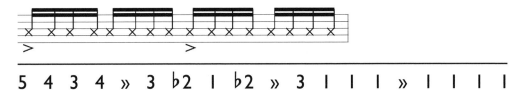

5  4  3  4  »  3  b2  1  b2  »  3  1  1  1  »  1  1  1  1

## 17. Cape Breton

8  1  1  b7  »  1  1  b6  1  \\  1  5  1  1  »  5  4  5  b7

## 18. Flamenco

1  b2  ♮3  »  8  8  \\  8·  »  b7  8  \\  b9  5  »  3  »  b2  4 »  {b2 » b2}
3  »  b2  »  1

## 19. Mariachi

I » b3 5 \\ b6 5 » 4 b6 » 5 4 » {5 \\ 5 I} b3 5 » 6 5
» 4 b3 » 2 **7** » I

## 20. Swedish

**7** I » **7** I » **7** I 2 b3 » 4 5 \\ b3 I

## 21. Bossa Nova

{4. 4} » 4 4 » {b7 \\ b7.} b7 » b6 b7 b6 \\ {b10. b9} b10. b9
» 8

## 22. Hungarian

b3 2 \\ 4 b3 2 I » 2 b3 » 4 b3 2 \\ I

## 23. Gypsy

2 {2 » 2 4 b3 2} » I **7** I 2 » b3 2 I **7** » I

## 24. Tango

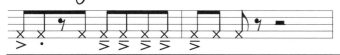

5 5 » b6 » 5 4 » b3 2 » I **5** » I

Most—though not all—of the examples in the next section are cadences, i.e. riffs consisting of a sequence of notes that indicate the momentary or actual end of a phrase or piece of music. Here are some ideas you can apply as you work on the riffs in this section:

## THREADING THE ENDING OF THE RIFF

If you want to have some **creative** fun with any of the riffs you work on, try adding a figure to the end of the riff that will naturally lead to the next key.

Remember, there are a number of methods you can use to navigate through the twelve keys:

◇ Cycle (move down in fifths or up in fourths) through the twelve keys.

◇ Chromatic Motion (half-step motion) ascending or descending.

◇ Whole Tone Motion (whole steps) ascending or descending.

◇ Diminished Motion (minor thirds) ascending or descending.

Let's say you decide to move the example below—or any riff—through the twelve keys and want to build in a transition. First, note the degree of the scale the riff starts and ends on. This riff starts on the fifth degree of the key and ends on the tonic (the root of the key):

C (1), D (2), E (3), F (4), **G (5th degree)**

*Riff 25*

If you decide to move up chromatically through the keys, you'll have to decide ahead of time whether you want to move the riff into the key of C♯, with a key signature of seven sharps, or D♭, a key signature with five flats, before you modulate up a half step from the key of C.

Then, you'll need to figure out an appealing way to lead seamlessly from the last note of the riff, the root of C—which is the C note—to the fifth of the key of D♭—the A♭ note:

D♭ (1), E♭ (2), F (3), G♭ (4), **A♭ (5th degree)**.

There are many ways to thread from the key of C to the Key of D♭. Here are two examples:

**Example One:**

**Example Two:**

On the other hand, if you decide you want to cycle down in fifths, you'll need to come up with an entirely different idea to move from a C note to the fifth degree of the key of F…a C again! This presents a new challenge.

For instance:

## CREATING VARIATIONS ON A RIFF

Once you feel comfortable with a riff you like, and can move it through the twelve keys as you hear, visualize, and track the interval relationships, you can use the riff as a tool to develop your compositional—and improvisational—skills. Let's explore this with a popular ragtime cadence.

*Riff 26*

This particular riff starts on the root of the key and winds its way down to end an octave lower on the root of the key.

Your objective will be to use elements from the riff in combination with new elements that fulfill the same—or close to it—contour of the line.

Here are two examples:

**Example One:**

**Example Two:**

You can play the following group of riffs as written for twelve-key motion, or toy with the ideas we've just discussed before moving them through the keys.

> **BOLD** = pitch can be found below the root.
> Brackets {5 5 4} = figure spans two beats.
> Arrows ( » ») separate beats.
> Backward double slash \\ separates measures.

# Blues, Jazz & Pop Riffs ♮♭♯

## Riff 27

**7** 2 4 » b6 b7 b6 » 5 4 » 3

## Riff 28

5 b5 4 1 » b3 b3 » 1

## Riff 29

b5 ♮5 \\ 1 8 3 4 » b5 ♮5

## Riff 30

**5** **b7** b3 » 1 1 b3 1 » b3 1 \\ /4 b3 \\ 1 1 b3 1 » b3 1

## Riff 31

5 b5 4 » b3 {♮3 » ♮3} 1 » **6** » 1

## Riff 32

5  6  5  »  b5  6  »  5  **7**  l  4  \\  3  **5**  **7**  2  »  l

## Riff 33

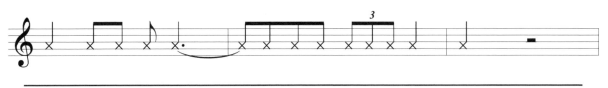

8  »  6  5  »  {l  3  »  3}  **5**  »  **6**  l  »  b3  2  l  »  **6**  \\  **5**

## Riff 34

l  2  »  3  5  6  »  b10  l  \\  l  2  »  3  5  6  »  b10  l  b7

## Riff 35

**6**  l  2  b3  »  2  l  **6**  5  »  **6**  l  2  b3  »  2  l  **6**  5  \\  l  b**7**  l

## Riff 36

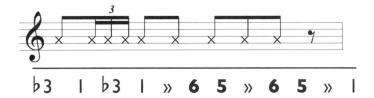

b3  l  b3  l  »  **6**  5  »  **6**  5  »  l

## Riff 87

8  7  »  b7  2  »  6  5  \\  8  7  »  b7  9  »  6  5

## Riff 88

**5**  I  »  3  5  »  4  I  »  2  {3  »  3}

## Riff 39

**5**  **6**  I  »  3  5  »  b3

## Riff 40

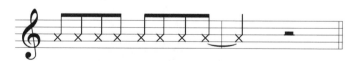

3  I  »  4  b5  »  ♮5  3  I  {b7  »  b7}

# Notated Versions of the Riffs

As discussed earlier, the brain isn't interested in rewiring! It will materialize every magic trick available to drive you back to the skills you've already mastered so it can economize energy by "taking a nap."

If you've skipped past the numbered examples on the previous pages to turn to these notated examples, you might be turning to the skills you've already cultivated and therefore feel more secure with. Consider alternating practice sessions: the numbering system on one day, notated examples the next.

On the other hand, if you've given it your best try and want to see how you did, then this section will help you double-check your efforts before you start to move your chosen phrase through the twelve keys.

---

**Please Note:** *Each example on the following pages is* **NOT** *notated in its original key. All phrases have been transposed to concert C to provide a start point before you move the phrase through all twelve keys,*

---

# Classical Riffs

## 1. Mozart

## 2. Bach

## 3. Vivaldi

## 4. Beethoven

## AMERICAN ROOTS RIFFS

## 5. Appalachian Fiddle Tag

## 6. Cajun

## 7. Bluegrass

## 8. Western Swing

## 9. Franco-American

# WORLD MUSIC RIFFS

## 10. Irish

## 11. Scottish

## 12. Klezmer

### 13. Cape Verde

### 14. Afro-Cuban

### 15. West African Kora

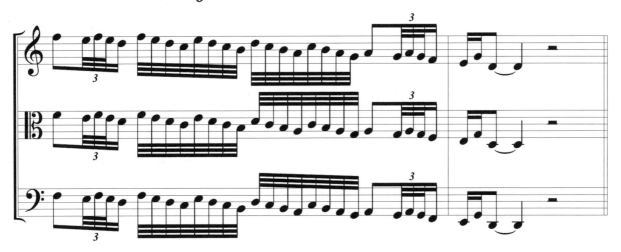

## 16. East Indian

## 17. Cape Breton

## 18. Flamenco

## 19. Mariachi

## 20. Swedish

## 21. Bossa Nova

## 22. Hungarian

## 23. Gypsy

## 24. Tango

# Blues, Jazz, and Pop Riffs

 Riff 25

Riff 26

 Riff 27

## Riff 28

## Riff 29

## Riff 30

## Riff 31

## Riff 32

## Riff 33

## Riff 84

## Riff 85

## Riff 86

## Riff 87

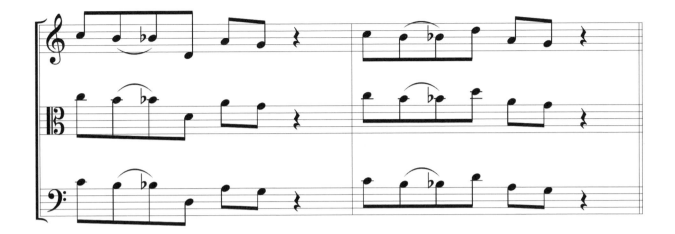

## Riff 38

## Riff 89

## Riff 40

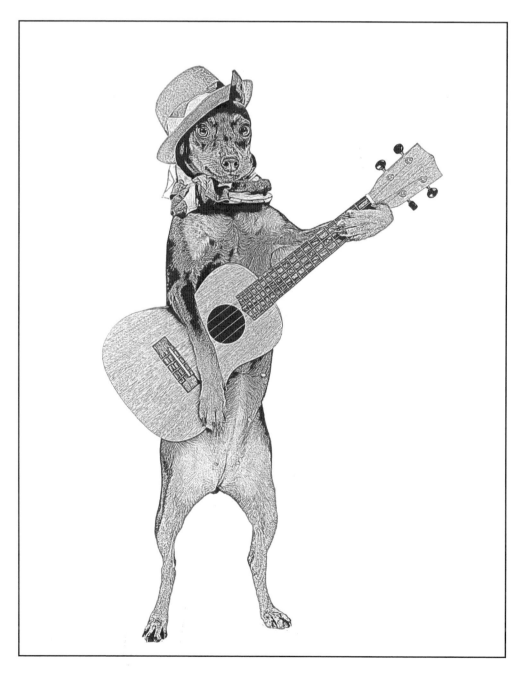

# What is a Scale... Really?

Traditionally, scales have been viewed as a family of five to seven pitches played from the root to the octave and back. This makes it easy to locate where you are within the context of each key. Some scale books add a little flourish, like repeating the first two notes or dipping down one to rev your way on up. The Twelve-Key approach presents a broader view, one that focuses on the concept of a continuous map so you are no longer root-bound and therefore don't need to practice from a fixed start-point that travels to its mirror an octave higher before the return to home base.

When you practice patterns that move from the lowest pitch on your instrument up to the highest within the scope of your technique, it's more challenging. This approach requires visualizing a map of the pitches and makes it more difficult to rely on your ears but ensures full command over each map. How, then, should you hold the notes in your mind and ears? What's the best protocol to apply to practice? Over the years, I've provided numerous exercises in private lesson and earlier books to help steer students toward alternative practice techniques. Patterns, like some of the following, more common examples, are certainly helpful, particularly when practiced without sheet music. You can also make up your own.

If you're going to practice scales in a linear manner, try moving octave-to-octave from each note of the scale because you're less likely to rely on your ears and more likely to picture the notes of the key across the range of your instrument. For instance, I call the following approach, "Waterfall Scales."

The goal of most repetitive practice is to teach each musical pattern to the brain. What if you teach your brain first? Less injury, less time, but greater concentration will be required.

*Note: If you want to heighten the challenge and therefore deepen mastery, try singing the scale and/or pattern of your choice as you name fingerings and pitches.*

# Common Ground

Ethnomusicologists define each semi-tone (half step) as divided into one hundred units, called "cents." This makes it easier to identify tuning systems from other cultures.

In the next few pages, we will spotlight traits shared by scales/maps throughout the world. In order to identify common ground, we will put aside cultural differences when it comes to discrepancies between tuning systems. For instance, in my book *Planet Musician*, scales from other tuning systems are conveyed by using (-) and (+) with an estimate of the number of cents in order to communicate the tuning system used by other cultures.

(-14)     (+9)

Later in this chapter, you will find fifty scales from around the world. **Most scales worldwide are made up of three intervals: half steps, whole steps, and minor thirds.** A small percentage also contain a gap of a perfect fourth (two and one-half steps).

For our purposes, we will focus on these three important intervals in order to master common ground. We'll use the system discussed earlier: **permutation**s.

Earlier in the book, we approached permutations as applied to pitch. Remember how we combined the first three pitches in a C major scale every possible way?

We will now apply this system to master half and whole steps as well as minor thirds in three-note groupings.

*Note: Once you can hear, visualize and recognize these units in any context, you will have the tools needed to master scales from all over the world almost instantaneously.*

# Permutations

As you work on gaining mastery over these three pivotal intervals, your goal should remain the same:

⬥ Hear the next interval before you play it.

⬥ Visualize the motion on your instrument before you move your body.

⬥ Play each combination while cognizant of the relationships.

## GROUPS OF TWO: HALF AND WHOLE STEPS

Notice how we've singled out two relationships in this first exercise, **half** and **whole steps**. They have been coupled every possible way.

**Half » Half**

**Whole » Whole**

**Half » Whole**

**Whole » Half**

# GROUPS OF TWO: HALF STEPS AND MINOR THIRDS

**Half » Half**

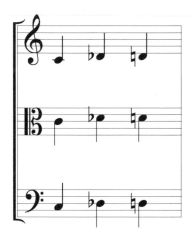

**Minor Third » Minor Third**

**Half » Minor Third**

**Minor Third » Half**

# GROUPS OF TWO: WHOLE STEPS AND MINOR THIRDS

You'll find that you've already mastered some of the following combinations from previous couplings.

### Whole » Whole

### Minor Third » Minor Third

### Whole » Minor Third

### Minor Third » Whole

# GROUPS OF THREE: HALF, WHOLE AND MINOR THIRDS

You will build your ear training skills and mental stamina by applying permutations to all three intervals. Take a moment to consider how you would organize permutations in all twelve keys. The goal is to avoid repeating the same combinations.

The system of organization presented here is based on every possible combination that starts with the first interval, a half step. Then, every combination that starts with a whole step. And, finally, with a minor third. But there is no right or wrong approach. You'll get more out of this practice if you use the following pages as guidelines and organize the material for yourself.

We'll now only use shorthand rather than music notation to represent these combinations:

**H = half step**          **W = whole step**          **m3 = minor third**

Choose a key and build these intervals from the root note. Then, apply this practice through the twelve keys.

1.  **H » W » m3**          4.  **W » H » m3**

2.  **H » m3 » W**          5.  **m3 » H » W**

3.  **W » m3 » H**          6.  **m3 » W » H**

## FOUR-NOTE COMBINATIONS

When you catalogue four-note combinations, the possibilities multiply because we have three intervals and one of them will have to be repeated somewhere within the order you determine. This pursuit could produce at least fifty-five combinations.

**It's your turn!** Try penciling in as many possible variations as you can that start with two whole steps. You should be able to find at least five. Can you hear and visualize each before playing it? Continue working on four-note permutations by choosing which of our three intervals (half, whole, and minor third) you will start with, then play second, third and fourth.

| | | |
|---|---|---|
| 1.  **W » W » ? » ?** | 1.  **h » h » ? » ?** | 1.  **m3 » m3 » ? » ?** |
| 2.  **W » W » ? » ?** | 2.  **h » h » ? » ?** | 2.  **m3 » m3 » ? » ?** |
| 3.  **W » W » ? » ?** | 3.  **h » h » ? » ?** | 3.  **m3 » m3 » ? » ?** |
| 4.  **W » W » ? » ?** | 4.  **h » h » ? » ?** | 4.  **m3 » m3 » ? » ?** |
| 5.  **W » W » ? » ?** | 5.  **h » h » ? » ?** | 5.  **m3 » m3 » ? » ?** |

The good news here is that once you've learned to hear, visualize, and track the interval relationships we've just covered, it's not that difficult to expand to a seven-note scale because you are really topping off your bottom three notes with one of the configurations we've just covered. Think of it like ordering an ice-cream cone with two scoops. Let's say your first scoop on the cone is made up of **h — m3 — h**. Then, for your second scoop, you add **W — W — h — W**.

Voila, you've just constructed a scale from at least two regions of the world, if not more: Eastern Europe or East India!

As you can see, the possibilities seem infinite and we haven't even worked our way up to groups of five notes, six and seven. If you've been weaned on Western canon, which only acknowledges major scales (**W » W » H » W » W » W » H**) and minor scales, of which there are four, you may already feel overwhelmed at this point. And we have fifty other scales just around the corner.

**Is it important to be able to identify where each scale comes from?** Yes, if that's the genre you wish to master. But for our purposes, we aren't going to focus on point of origin. **The key focus here, is on the relationship between pitches, on the ability to hear and visualize as well as play any grouping of notes with accuracy in all twelve keys.**

Now, compare this fully engaged learning process to reading notated exercises start to finish while thinking about something else. Like what you're going to have for lunch or who you forgot to text as you automatically play what you see on the music stand or repeat the same warm-up exercises you've played for days, weeks, or even years. "Zzzzzzz," says your brain. "Zzzzzzz," say your ears. "Sure," your body replies… "play it a few more times and I, too, can go to sleep."

To clear your mind and clarify your history before you take a peek at *Fifty World Maps*, take a moment and pencil in the half and whole steps that make up the following four scales: natural minor, harmonic minor, melodic minor and Dorian minor.

*Write out the degrees of the natural minor scale using the numbering system.*

Write out the degrees of the Harmonic Minor scale using the numbering system.

Write out the degrees of the Melodic Minor scale using the numbering system.

Write out the degrees of the Dorian Minor scale using the numbering system.

# Fifty World Maps

We would need an entire book to cover every single scale ever invented by each country in the world. The following thesaurus of scales will keep you busy for several lifetimes. Particularly if you practice each scale through all twelve keys.

These maps have been loosely organized with no particular hierarchy in mind beyond demonstrating the innumerable possibilities as it applies to the human musical imagination. Some cultures employ scales with fewer than seven notes, while others use more. And not all cultures agree that every pitch deserves equal emphasis. Only a sample have been included on the following pages.

## SUGGESTED PRACTICE APPROACH

In accordance with how we've approached the riff collection, you might consider perusing the scale collection to find a map that's new to you. Then break it down into manageable segments. For instance, if the upper portion is familiar to you, like 4 5 ♭6 ♭7 8, but the lower section starts out with 1 ♭2 3, you might consider breaking it down into two Kaleis:

- ◇ Play root to flatted second and move through the twelve keys.

- ◇ Play root, flatted second, major third through the twelve keys.

At the risk of sounding like a broken record, use the twelve-key practice approach as your standard of measurement for mastery!

Audiate each interval before you play it. Visualize the motion on your instrument before you move your fingers and/or lips. Make sure you can name the notes as you play them before you move to the next key.

**These maps have been notated two ways:**

- ◇ With the degrees of the scale.

- ◇ With traditional notation.

# Maps by Degree: Seven Pitches, Plus...

1.   1 » 2 » 3 » 4 » 5 » 6 » 7 » 8

2.   1 » 2 » ♭3 » 4 » 5 » 6 » ♭7 » 8

3.   1 » 2 » ♭3 » 4 » 5 » 6 » ♭7 » 8

4.   1 » 2 » 3 » 4 » 5 » ♭6 » ♭7 » 8

5.   1 » 2 » ♭3 » 4 » 5 » ♭6 » ♭7 » 8

6.   1 » ♭2 » ♭3 » 4 » 5 » ♭6 » ♭7 » 8

7.   1 » ♭2 » ♭3 » 4 » ♭5 » ♭6 » ♭7 » 8

8.   1 » ♭2 » ♭3 » ♭4 » ♭5 » ♭6 » ♭7 » 8

9.   1 » 2 » 3 » ♯4 » 5 » 6 » 7 » 8

10.  1 » 2 » 3 » ♯4 » ♯5 » 6 » 7 » 8

11.  1 » 2 » 3 » ♯4 » ♯5 » ♯6 » 8

12.  1 » 2 » 3 » ♯4 » 5 » 6 » ♭7 » 8

13.  1 » 2 » ♭3 » #4 » 5 » 6 » 7 » 8

14.  1 » ♭2 » 3 » #4 » 5 » 6 » 7 » 8

15.  1 » ♭2 » 3 » #4 » 5 » ♭6 » 7 » 8

16.  1 » ♭2 » ♭3 » #4 » 5 » ♭6 » 7 » 8

17.  1 » ♭2 » 3 » 4 » 5 » ♭6 » 7 » 8

18.  1 » 2 » 4 » #4 » 5 » 6 » 7 » 8

19.  1 » 2 » ♭3 » 3 » 4 » 5 » 6 » 8

20.  1 » ♭3 » #4 » 5 » ♭6 » ♭7 » 8

21.  1 » ♭2 » ♭3 » #4 » 5 » ♭6 » ♭7 » 8

22.  1 » ♭2 » 2 » 4 » #4 » #5 » 6 » 8

23.  1 » ♭2 » ♭3 » 3 » 5 » ♭6 » ♭7 » 8

24.  1 » 2 » 4 » #4 » 5 » ♭7 » 7 » 8

25.  1 » ♭2 » ♭3 » #4 » 5 » #5 » 6 » 8

26.    1 » ♭2 » 2 » 4 » 5 » #5 » 6 » 8

27.    1 » ♭2 » 3 » 4 » 5 » 6 » ♭7 » 8

28.    1 » ♭2 » 3 » 4 » 5 » ♭6 » ♭7 » 8

29.    1 » 2 » ♭3 » #4 » 5 » 6 » ♭7 » 8

30.    1 » 2 » ♭3 » 4 » 5 » ♭7 » 7 » 8

31.    1 » 2 » ♭3 » 4 » 5 » ♭6 » 7 » 8

32.    1 » ♭2 » ♭3 » 3 » #4 » 5 » 6 » ♭7 » 8

33.    1 » ♭2 » ♭3 » 3 » #4 » 5 » 6 » 7 » 8

34.    1 » ♭2 » 2 » ♭3 » 3 » 4 » 5 » 7 » 8

## MAPS BY DEGREE: FIVE PITCHES

35.    1 » 2 » 4 » 5 » ♭7 » 8

36.    1 » 2 » ♭3 » 5 » ♭6 » 8

37.    1 » ♭2 » 4 » 5 » ♭6 » 8

38.　| » ♭2 » 4 » ♭5 » ♭7 » 8

39.　| » 2 » ♭3 » 5 » 6 » 8

40.　| » ♭3 » 4 » 5 » ♭7 » 8

41.　| » 3 » 4 » 5 » ♭6 » 8

42.　| » 2 » ♯4 » 5 » 6 » 8

43.　| » ♭3 » 4 » ♭5 » ♭7 » 8

44.　| » ♭2 » ♭3 » 5 » ♭7 » 8

45.　| » 2 » ♭3 » ♯4 » 6 » 8

46.　| » ♭2 » 4 » 5 » ♭6 » 8

47.　| » ♭2 » 4 » 5 » 6 » 8

48.　| » 2 » 3 » 5 » 6 » 8

49.　| » 2 » ♭3 » 5 » 6 　　8

50.　| » 2 » 3 » ♯4 » 6 » 8

# Notated Maps

**1.**

**2.**

**3.**

**4.**

**5.**

**6.**

**7.**

**8.**

**9.**

**10.**

**11.**

**12.**

**13.**

**14.**

**15.**

**16.**

**17.**

**18.**

**19.**

**20.**

**21.**

**22.**

**23.**

**24.**

25.

26.

27.

28.

29.

30.

**31.**

**32**

**33.**

**84.**

**35.**

**86.**

**37.**

**38.**

**39.**

**40.**

**41.**

**42**

**43.**

**44.**

**45.**

**46.**

**47.**

**48.**

# Paradiddles ♭♭#

Drummers use the term "paradiddle" to refer to two single strokes with one hand, followed by a double stroke with the other: RLRR or LRLL, for example. In this section, we will borrow from that concept by focusing on an interplay between two pitches—or more—to create an intriguing pattern of activity without the traditional approach to melody. These patterns have been culled from a number of world styles.

> The paradiddle reveals how we can create a great deal of intrigue out of very few pitches.

You may wonder what paradiddles have to do with the twelve-key approach. As you master the ability to hear, visualize, and analyze each world scale provided in this section in order to move it through the twelve keys, we are still in pursuit of constantly heightened mental and physical challenges to increase musical mastery.

When you add a paradiddle into the equation, you are like a juggler who's transitioned from juggling three or four balls to five or six. In fact, you're now equal to the *Flying Karamazov Brothers*. Most jugglers juggle like with like: balls, clubs, or rings. But the brothers were known for juggling items from the audience. For instance, a set of keys, a heavy chain, and a jacket!

Let's take a look at how you might integrate any paradiddle into your scale practice. Here's a before and after for each. Both are suggestions. The idea is for you to figure out your own unique application.

*Scale #21.*

*Paradiddle #7.*

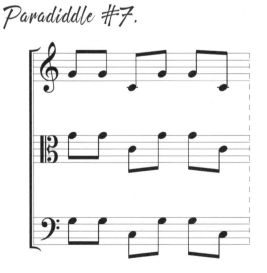

Since most paradiddles don't neatly tuck into 4/4 time, this example aptly demonstrates how focused your ears and mind must be to track the notes of the scale and the paradiddle simultaneously—without the benefit of a symmetrical shape to the rhythmic interplay of each two notes. In fact, this particular paradiddle requires three measures to come back around to the downbeat on the first beat of the measure.

When you widen the gap between the two alternating notes, you can immediately transform the nature of the challenge. For instance, you might decide to alternate with the top note of the scale rather than pitches that are side-by-side. Here's an excerpt to demonstrate that practice approach:

The following paradiddles demonstrate a range of possibilities. Let's see what you come up with to further the challenge even more!

---

*Note: If a paradiddle ends with a rest, replace the rest(s) by starting the paradiddle from the beginning again. This displaces its position across the downbeats and makes for an incredibly dynamic sound when playing with a rhythm section.*

---

# TWELVE PARADIDDLES

**1.**

**2.**

**3.**

**4.**

**5.**

**6.**

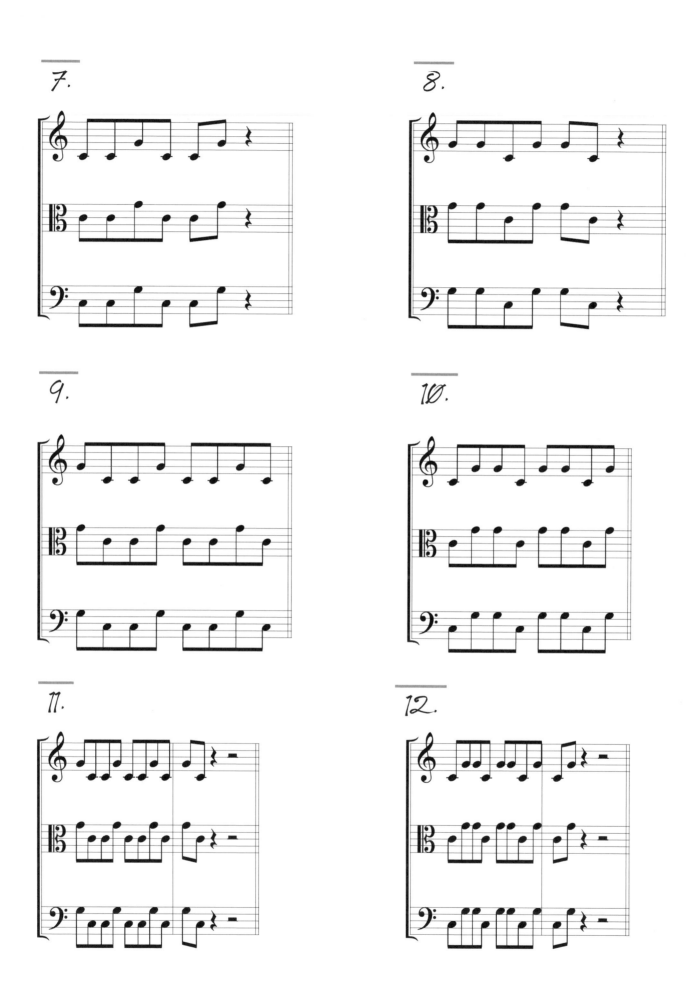

# The Rhythmic Side of the Equation

All too often, musicians practice scales using symmetrical rhythms, like quarter notes or eighth notes. This provides an opportunity to focus exclusively on the pitches. That's appropriate, particularly for scales and keys you don't yet feel comfortable with. However, when you compare the time each year you practice pitch sequences versus rhythmic, you will most likely find that your *rhythmic brain* is not receiving dedicated practice time equal to your *melodic brain*. How about if you treat yourself to the best of both worlds? Warm up on a new scale and then apply a new rhythm to each note of the scale to "flex" the rhythmic part of the brain.

> The part of the brain that processes pitch is actually in a different location from the part of the brain that processes rhythm.

As with the scale collection, our purpose here is to heighten rhythmic skill by tapping into the musical imagination of the world. Here are two practice techniques you can apply:

- ◇ Clap, tap, or play each rhythm on a single pitch to hone your rhythmic skills. A rhythmic accompaniment from the metronome or backing track can help ensure accuracy.

- ◇ Focus on a rhythmic figure that's new to you and apply it to each note of the scale you are currently practicing.

For instance, here's an example of scale #28 as quarter notes, and then again with rhythm #8.

First, the rhythm is applied to each note of the scale to lock in the union between the two. This approach ensures the ability to relax while joining them together, as well as to hear, visualize and analyze degrees and relationships.

You can apply a Kalei to this process by cycling over a small nugget of terrain first.

If that's going well for you, try changing pitch in tandem with each rhythmic value:

Now apply the rhythm and scale of your choice to all twelve keys.

Each culture has developed its own unique spin on how to subdivide notes in a measure. A seemingly simple stream of eighth notes or triplets can sound entirely different depending on the placement of accents, rests or ties. As is the case with the scale collection, the following rhythmic examples only represent a fraction of possibilities, but should provide ample material for you to work with to super-boost your rhythmic skills.

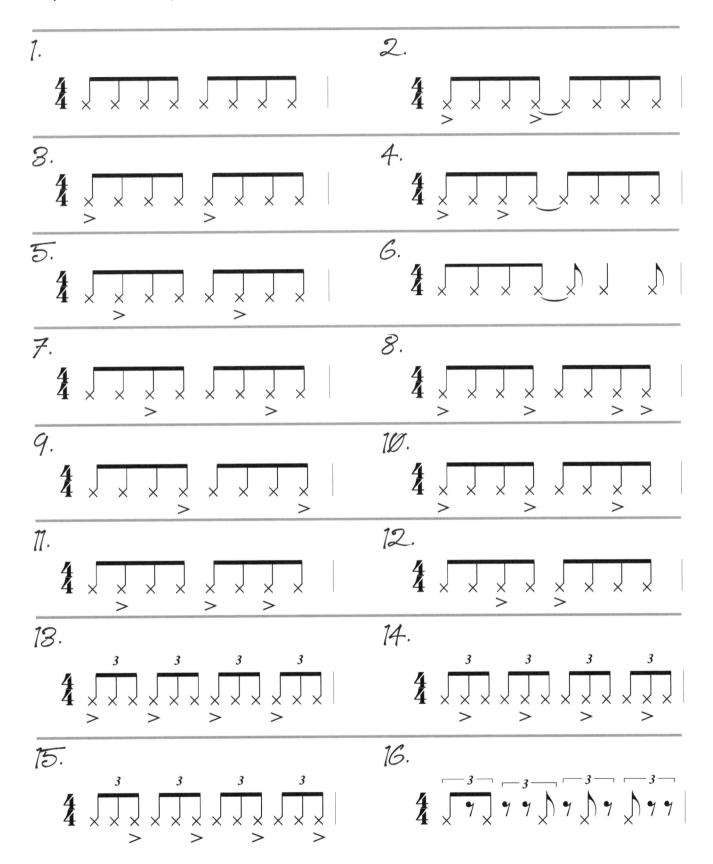

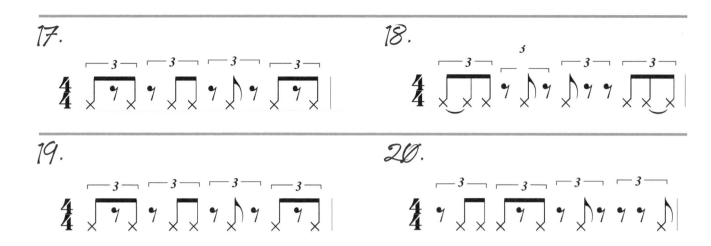

The following examples include syncopated and dotted rhythmic phrases.

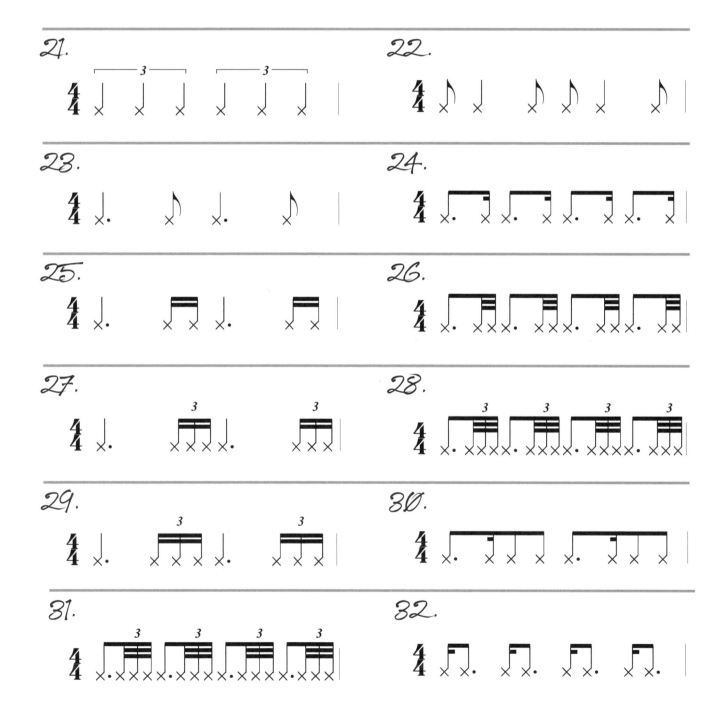

This next series of rhythmic phrases demonstrates combinations of rhythmic values. You've worked with permutations throughout the book, so by now you know you can combine any of the ideas in this entire unit to build more complex rhythmic phrases. Your tools include the **basic rhythms** (quarter, eighth, triplet, etc.), **dots**, **slurs**, **ties**, **ornaments** and **accents**.

There is a secondary benefit to isolating any rhythmic phrase that's outside your wheelhouse and applying it repetitively to the notes of a scale or pattern. If you're an improvising musician, you might tend to only play the rhythms you're familiar with and begin to bore yourself. This practice approach will help broaden your vocabulary.

If you can hear it, you can—and will—play it with ease.

# A Message from Julie

Musicians rarely settle. We constantly pursue greater skill. Not for its own sake, but to further our ability to create art... to build something from nothing out of the mystery of the imagination. Do we need to create music as much as we need oxygen and food? Actually... yes!

Culture. Civilization. Society. Empty and meaningless without art. Music bypasses the world of words to transform and elevate the human spirit.

Thank you for sharing this journey with me.

JULIE LYONN LIEBERMAN is a multi-style improvising violinist, fiddler, vocalist, clinician, author and composer. She has performed throughout the United States as well as in Canada and Europe, and has played on and off-Broadway, in folk and jazz clubs, as well as on radio and TV.

She is the author of eight music books and six educational DVDs, as well as over two-dozen string orchestra scores in American and world styles (Carl Fischer, Kendor and Alfred Music). She has also co-written and co-produced two National Public Radio Series: *The Talking Violin*, hosted by Dr. Billy Taylor, and *Jazz Profiles: Jazz Violin* hosted by Nancy Wilson with famed radio producer Steve Rathe.

She is the recipient of the 2014 American String Teachers Association (ASTA) Kudos Award, over two-dozen ASCAP Plus Awards, eight Meet the Composer awards and three American String Teachers Association's National Citation for Leadership & Merit awards.

She's been on faculty as an adjunct at The Juilliard School, The New School for Jazz and Contemporary Music, William Paterson College Jazz Department, Manhattan School of Music, New York University's Gallatin Division, VanderCook College of Music, and Mercy College. In addition, she has worked as a guest clinician at the Eastman School of Music, National String Workshop, International String Workshop, Stanford Jazz Workshop, and many other schools and program across the United States, in Canada, and abroad.

JULIE LYONN LIEBERMAN is also the Artistic Director for the summer program, *Strings Without Boundaries* and has played an active role in the promotion of American and world styles in music education for over forty years as a performer, clinician, author, composer, radio and concert producer, and recording artist. Ms. Lieberman is also an NS Design Performance Artist and a D'Addario Premiere Clinician.

# Resources by Julie Lyonn Lieberman

## BOOKS

*Planet Musician*

*You Are Your Instrument*

*Creative Band and Orchestra*

*Rockin' Out with Blues Fiddle*

*Improvising Violin*

*The Contemporary Violinist*

*Alternative Styles: The New Curriculum*

*How to Play Contemporary Strings*

## DVDs

*Vocal Aerobics*

*The Violin in Motion*

*Vioin and Viola Ergonomics*

*Techniques for the Contemporary String Player*

*Rhythmizing the Bow*